D1370254

PUBLIC RELATIONS

 made easy

Additional Titles in Entrepreneur's MADE EASY Series

- *Business Plans Made Easy,* Third Edition by David H. Bangs, Jr.
- *Nonprofits Made Easy* by David H. Bangs, Jr.
- *Direct Response Advertising Made Easy* by Roscoe Barnes III
- *Managing a Small Business Made Easy* by Martin E. Davis
- *Business Models Made Easy* by Don Debelak
- *Marketing Made Easy* by Kevin A. Epstein
- *Strategic Planning Made Easy* by Fred L. Fry, Charles R. Stoner, and Laurence G. Weinzimmer
- *Mastering Business Growth and Change Made Easy* by Jeffrey A. Hansen
- *Project Management Made Easy* by Sid Kemp
- *Advertising Without an Agency Made Easy* by Kathy J. Kobliski
- *Customer Service Made Easy* by Paul Levesque
- *Accounting and Finance for Small Business Made Easy: Secrets You Wish Your CPA Had Told You* by Robert Low
- *Meetings Made Easy: The Ultimate Fix-It Guide* by Frances Micale

Entrepreneur
MAGAZINE'S

PUBLIC RELATIONS

made easy

Entrepreneur Press and
Roscoe Barnes III

EP
Entrepreneur® Press

Editorial Director: Jere Calmes
Cover Design: Beth Hansen-Winter
Editorial and Production Services: CWL Publishing Enterprises, Inc., Madison,
Wisconsin, www.cwlpub.com

This publication is designed to provide accurate and authoritative information in
regard to the subject matter covered. It is sold with the understanding that the
publisher is not engaged in rendering legal, accounting, or other professional services. If legal advice or other expert assistance is required, the services of a compe-
tent professional person should be sought.

> —From a Declaration of Principles jointly adopted by
> a Committee of the American Bar Association and
> a Committee of Publishers and Associations

ISBN 13: 978-1-59918-078-6
       10: 1-59918-078-2

Library of Congress Cataloging-in-Publication Data

Barnes, Roscoe, 1961-
  Public relations made easy / by Entrepreneur Press and Roscoe Barnes III.
    p. cm.
  ISBN-13: 978-1-59918-078-6 (alk. paper)
  ISBN-10: 1-59918-078-2 (alk. paper)
  1. Public relations. 2. Mass media and business. 3. Press releases.
4. Publicity I. Entrepreneur Press. II. Title.
HD59.B354 2007
  659.2—dc22
Printed in Canada   2007002464

10 09 08 07 06   10 9 8 7 6 5 4 3 2 1

Dedication

I dedicate this book to my mother, Bertha M. Barnes, my oldest sister,
Alberta Harrington, and my oldest brother, Wiley Barnes.
Together, they have taught me the value of love,
family and hard work.

Contents

Contents

Introduction

What You Can Expect from This Book

A SINGLE CHAPTER IN THIS BOOK CAN HELP YOU GENERATE THOU-sands of dollars in free publicity on a local, regional or national level.

The purpose of this book is clear: It is designed to help you snag media attention and stir up interest in your business without the aid of a publicist or public relations firm.

As an award-winning journalist with over 20 years of newspaper experience, I have personally reviewed and edited thousands of press releases and other publicity related documents. I have also conducted thousands of interviews for newspapers and magazines. In this book, for the first time, I draw on this experience as a reporter and pull the curtain back, to let the business world know what it takes to succeed with the news media.

This unique resource provides you with everything you need to know in order to launch—and sustain—a successful publicity campaign. Written from the perspective of a veteran newsman, it reveals in plain language how to woo the press and stir up interest in your products, services, name, or business. It uses concise tips and proven tactics that will help you generate thousands of dollars worth of free publicity, all without the help of a publicist or PR firm.

Unlike other books that offer theory and hype, and often require hours to read, this book provides you with the ideas that matter—and practical advice that actually works. Modeled after *The Elements of Style*, it is an indispensable quick-reference guide for entrepreneurs, marketers, or any small business. As such, it trims the fat off of facts and gives you exactly what you need to immediately begin a solid campaign. In addition to advice based on real-life experience, this reader-friendly guide introduces you to the essential tools for working with the media. Everything is covered, including how to write and design press kits, press releases, pitch letters, postcards, newsletters, and slogans. Other topics include:

▶ how to promote through public speaking

▶ how to write columns for the local press

▶ how to become a nationally known expert in your field

Also included are sample documents, checklists, and a list of recommended resources.

You will note that special emphasis is given to *news* and what it means to editors and reporters. That's because a successful publicity campaign is all about news and persistence. An effective campaign can be launched on a shoestring by any small business without the high cost of hiring a publicist or PR firm.

The primary market for this book consists of small business owners and managers, copywriters, and entrepreneurs. Others who would find this book useful are: students, creative directors, consultants, marketing directors, communication directors, public relations and publicity coordinators, and account executives.

Whether you run a commercial enterprise or a non-profit organization, the tips and ideas presented here will help you to generate tons of publicity. Your name, products, services, or political agenda, can all receive news coverage on the local or national level. So read on and see how you and your business can use this information and shine in the media spot light.

Acknowledgments

The writing of this book was made possible primarily because of the training and experiences I've had as a journalist. For more than 20 years, I've worked with number of good newspapers and press associations. Because of the knowledge I gained under the tutelage of seasoned editors, it's only fitting that I recognize those who influenced me the most.

Therefore, I take pride in offering gratitude to Becky Bennett of *Public Opinion*, Sue Ernde Hadden, Scott Weaver, Denny Shockey, and Pat Patterson of *The Record Herald*, Jim Abbott and David Rushing of *The Enterprise-Tocsin*, Hal Sharpe of *The Littleton Observer*, B.J. Small and Robert Holt of *The Gettysburg Times*, Stan Schwartz of Publishers' Auxiliary, Gail Williams of *The Tidal Wave*, Denny and Peggy Hatch of Target Marketing, George Reis of Fund Raising Management, and Margaret Battistelli of *FundRaising Success*.

Grateful acknowledgments are made to a number of great copywriters and marketers who gave permission for the use of their work. They include: Beth Ann Erickson, Peter Fogel, Pam Lontos, Robert W. Bly, and Alan Lane.

Special thanks are owed to my friends, Leo Canseco, Greg Bolyard, Anna Dingle, Lisa Warfield, Lee Gray, and Carole Hunt. All of them have provided support and inspiration. Merritt Clifton, former publisher of Samisdat, was a big help in the early days of my career, along with Norman B. Rohrer, founder and former director of the Christian Writers Guild.

As always, I am especially grateful to my agent, Bob Diforio of D4EO Lterary Agency. He has been a tremendous blessing to me. I'm also grateful to my editor, Jere Calmes, and his assistant editor, Karen Thomas. Both of them have used their editorial and administrative magic to make his book a real treasure—and essential tool—for business people everywhere.

Finally, I want to thank John Woods and his staff at CWL Publishing for the great job they did in designing and producing the book as you now see it.

Chapter 1

The 22 Most Common Mistakes Made in Publicity Campaigns

Avoiding the Pitfalls and Land Mines that Can Waste Your Time and Hurt Your Budget

THE SURGERY WAS A SUCCESS," THE PROUD SURGEON SAID.
After spending several hours in the operating room, he finally stitched up the patient, and he and his team were reveling in their achievement. Everything was well. Or so they thought.

Two weeks later, the patient was back in the hospital after complaining about stomach pain. An x-ray revealed that a surgical instrument had been left inside him. What was believed to have been a successful operation turned out to be a nightmare for the surgeon, and for the hospital. This one mistake resulted in a lawsuit for millions of dollars.

Indeed mistakes can be costly. This is true in any endeavor, including public relations or publicity campaigns. Sometimes, what you think is a success could end up costing you and your business, all because of a mistake.

Experienced PR professionals know what to avoid when launching a campaign. Unfortunately, the same cannot be said of many entrepreneurs and small businesspeople who are just starting out. The good news is, you can learn from others and avoid the mistakes and frustrations that are so common in PR campaigns. Your success in this endeavor, however, must start with an awareness of what those mistakes are, and what you must do to prevent them.

The 22 Most Common Mistakes Made in Publicity Campaigns

Below is a list of the 22 most common mistakes made in publicity campaigns. Take a look and see if your work measures up. Make note of the problem areas and devise a plan to effectively deal with them. With this in mind, let's get started.

1. You have a "Field of Dreams" mentality.

You can build the best ball field, create the best mousetrap, but nobody will come unless you have a strong PR campaign.

"Field of Dreams," starring Kevin Costner, was a great flick with more than its share of inspiration. And the line, "If you build it, they will come," became known and often repeated by millions of adoring fans. While that powerful concept may work in the movie, it does not translate into success in business. This is especially true when you need and want publicity in order to sell more of your products and services.

In reality, you can build the best ball field, create the best mousetrap, or offer the best line of clothing, but nobody will come unless you have a strong PR campaign. Perhaps P.T. Barnum had it right when he said, "Without promotion, something terrible happens … Nothing!"

2. You omit real news when contacting the press.

This may well be the number one sin in public relations: You contact the press and offer hype, photos, cute stories, and everything else *but* news. Although newspapers have space for entertainment, letters, and cartoons, their biggest need is for news—information that provides something new, different, strange, useful, and important for their readers. Since news is the life-blood of the media, you would be wise to fill your publicity documents with enticing tidbits they will be eager to use.

Before you send out your next press release, ask yourself: What's new about this story? How does it differ from other stories? Why would the public be interested?

2

"I see two chronic mistakes most publicity-seekers make," says copywriter Beth Ann Erickson. "They don't make their press releases newsworthy, and they continually talk about themselves instead of the prospective reader."

Erickson, who is also author of *Jumpstart Your Writing Career and Snag Paying Assignments* (Kandiyohi, MN: Filbert Publishing, 2006), has a few more words about this topic. She writes:

> If you want free publicity, you have to make your announcement newsworthy. On the surface you're probably thinking, "duh." However, after freelancing at various newspapers and radio stations this past decade I can assure you that the VAST majority of press releases received by the organizations I've worked with have absolutely, positively nothing to do with news.
>
> Listen to a news broadcast. Have you EVER in your life heard the announcer say anything like, "Filbert Publishing celebrated its seventh anniversary"? I doubt you have. And if you did, either the news department is totally incompetent or it was an incredibly slow news day. The headline, "Filbert Publishing Celebrates Seventh Anniversary," is all about me and my company. Bad idea.

In the book, *Professional News Writing* (Lawrence Erlbaum Associates Inc., 1990), Bruce Garrison outlines a few characteristics of news. He notes that news involves:

1. **Timeliness:** It is relevant for the present and must be reported as soon as possible.
2. **Magnitude:** It has an impact on many people, particularly those in your audience.
3. **Proximity:** It hits home. In other words, it relates to people where they are and affects them in a direct way.
4. **Interest:** It is interesting, especially when it involves people. It must have a human dimension element.
5. **Drama:** It is compelling or it tells a story that can have a dramatic impact on readers or viewers. This includes accidents, pain, overcoming hardships, achievements.
6. **Prominence:** It features big names, big companies, big deeds, big schools, big achievements. This includes well-known personalities, politicians, business leaders, and sports figures.
7. **Conflict:** It includes two opposing forces at work to achieve a certain goal.

There are other characteristics mentioned by Garrison, but the ones listed here should give you a sense of what you need to feed the press.

3. You submit advertisements.

Editors and reporters can spot an advertisement a mile away. So it's a waste of time to write up an advertisement about your business and disguise it as a press release. When I worked for a community newspaper in Pennsylvania, my job entailed opening the daily mail to sort press releases and mail for our sales department. The press releases were placed in one pile, and advertisements in another pile. When I came across a fake release, I'd quickly forward it to our sales department. "Here's another one looking for ad space," I'd say.

If you want to befriend the media, it is critical to provide them with real news.

On rare occasions, if the "fake" document had a hint of news, I'd call up the business and ask a few questions to see if it had the potential for a story. If it did, I'd write up a short story without the superlatives and sales talk.

If you want to befriend the media, it is critical to provide them with real news. Do not play games in hopes of slipping an ad past them. Trust me, it could backfire.

4. You ignore protocol and guidelines.

Every business has certain protocols for communicating with customers. Newspapers are no exception. Therefore when contacting them for a story, you must meet their requirements—and follow their guidelines—in order to find print.

As a reporter, it was not unusual for a person to call me on deadline and ask for coverage of an event. Almost daily I received press releases that were single-spaced, hand-written, and without contact information. When my paper asked for news via snail mail, people continued to send their work by e-mail. Only a few actually read and followed the paper's guidelines.

If you're in doubt as to how to submit press documents to the local media, take a look at their web site. Check out their editorial page and masthead. Or, you can simply call and ask for their guidelines. Doing this will endear you to a busy editor or reporter.

5. Your press release is poorly written.

The less editing required for your press release, the greater your chances of seeing it published. More editing means more work, and sometimes, frustration, for over-worked editors.

No, you don't have to be an English major or hire a high-profile editor to review your work before submitting it. However, it would help to have a good proofreader. Ask him or her to check for accuracy, spelling, and good organization.

Remember to use a good headline that announces what the press release is about. Follow this with a lead paragraph that tells the who, what, why, when, where, and how about your topic. Include names with titles. And don't forget contact information.

Keep paragraphs and sentences as short as possible. Cut out most adjectives and rely on strong verbs. Cut out all words that suggest you're bragging about your company. Attribute all quotes and back up all claims. If you need help in this area, review a copy of the latest edition of *The Elements of Style* by William Strunk Jr. and E.B. White. This is one of the most useful books ever written about style. In fact, it has been the bible for writers and journalists for many decades. And, I'm sure, it will help you to improve not only your press documents, but any kind of writing you attempt. I try to read it at least once a year. You should do the same.

6. You leave out important contact information in your press release.

This may seem a minor point, but it's highly important to editors. If they have a question or want an interview, they need to reach you—ASAP.

As a reporter, I can recall many occasions when I wanted to reach someone after receiving a press release. Sometimes they would list a phone number on the release, but when I called, I found it to be a home number, but they were at work. Other times I'd call a number and find it to be a work number, but the person was at home. Usually when this happens, the press release is laid aside, along with the possibility for a story, until I can reach the person at a later time.

Be accessible at all times. Make it easy for a reporter to contact you.

To avoid this disappointing experience, always include *all* contact information. Be accessible at all times. Make it easy for a reporter to contact you. Do this by including your cell, home, and work phone numbers. Include a fax number along with your e-mail address and web site. Leave nothing to chance.

7. You fail to attribute sources in your press release.

It is best to avoid making wild claims in your press documents, but if you do—and they are true—be sure to provide proof. If you claim that your new product is being used by more athletes than any other similar product, back it up. If you say that you have the fastest turnaround on repairing vehicles, please explain how you reached this conclusion.

Often you hear (or read) such statements as, "New study shows this product will ...." Really? What study? If you write that "experts agree" your product will solve a certain problem or help your prospects save money, you should specifically name some of these experts.

As I write this, I'm thinking of a self-proclaimed marketing guru who promotes himself as one of the top five copywriters in the world. Now that's a pretty hefty claim, wouldn't you say? To his own detriment, this "guru" does not provide proof. While he may impress a few gullible people seeking get-rich-quick opportunities, his claim, for the most part, falls on deaf ears.

Make it a practice to always provide proof for your claims, and attribute all quotes and startling statements. Proof will lend credibility to your press documents and encourage editors to take you seriously.

8. Your press release is too long.

Telling your story in a brief, concise manner will save them time by allowing editors to assess the news merit of your piece with the blink of an eye.

Unless it is critically important and extremely captivating, a press release should only be one to two pages in length. Anything more is a waste of time and a sure-fire way to frustrate busy editors. Among other things, it suggests to them that you are not a professional. It also shows you are not clear about what you have to say.

Editors want to get the gist of your news in the first two paragraphs of your press release. Telling your story in a brief, concise manner will save them time by allowing them to assess the news merit of your piece with the blink of an eye. This also means they don't have to bother with cutting and revising in order to make the piece fit on their pages.

I remember the days at a certain small newspaper where we reporters would joke about long press releases. Because we had to type them into our computer system in preparation for page layout and design, none of us wanted to tackle them. Even worse, some of these documents were actually single-spaced, if you can believe it. Sometimes we'd hold up a three-pager and say, "Here's another book. Who wants it?"

9. You don't tailor your media documents to the right publications.

For the best results, your media documents have to fit the publications in which you want to be covered. "Always pitch a publication or program by highlighting the benefits your business can offer their particular audience," advises Pam Lontos of PrPr Public Relations. "Consider what uniqueness you can offer and why their readers or viewers will be interested in what you have to say."

Lontos, a highly successful PR professional, notes that the more you learn about the media's needs, and you customize your message for their specific audience, the more likely you'll be featured in their publication or on their show.

10. You don't make any free offers.

Mentioning a free offer is an effective way to turn your press release into a direct response tool. Besides allowing you to find prospects and develop your mailing list, it can lead to direct sales. Typically, this works by offering a free booklet, tip sheet, how-to guide, or newsletter. Because this offer is mentioned in the news section—and not an ad—readers are more likely to respond.

Mentioning a free offer is an effective way to turn your press release into a direct response tool.

Two approaches seem to work best with this method:

1. Write a standard release and mention the free offer at the bottom. Example: "For more information, call … "
2. Write the entire release about the free offer. In this case, you would start with the headline. Example: "New book shows gardeners how to raise giant tomatoes." From there you would offer a few tips.

When making a free offer, it's important to provide solid, how-to information that meets a need, and not a commercial. Although technically you are "selling," you don't want it to be obvious. So remove all commercial language in your document and avoid all bragging. Remember to focus on the audience.

I once tried this approach during a publicity campaign for my gospel tract ministry. In case you're wondering, "tracts" are little pamphlets with religious messages that are freely distributed by churches and individuals. Anyway, I wrote up a press release and included the offer of free tracts to anyone who requested them. I submitted this release to a denominational magazine. The editor turned the release into a feature story and included all contact information for the free offer. One week after it was published, I began receiving letters, e-mails, and phone calls from people all across the United States. In addition to building my mailing list, I also found financial contributors for my work. To my surprise, the article generated requests for over two years.

11. You don't follow up on your submissions and media requests.

As far as I'm concerned, follow-up is one of the silver bullets for success in any endeavor. In terms of public relations, it allows you to stay on top of your efforts. Even more, you get to communicate directly with your media contacts. Besides this, it can actually lead to the publication of your press releases.

So if you submit a request or a release to the media, it's OK to follow up and inquire about its status. No need to bug the editor by calling every week. With your first call, you can ask the editor if she received the document. If she has, then ask if she has any questions or needs more information. Chances are she will let you know if or when she will run your release. If she doesn't, then it's OK to ask. Just do so without being pushy.

If you submit a request or a release to the media, it's OK to follow up and inquire about its status.

My belief in the value of follow-up was reinforced by an experience I had with *Soldiers* magazine. A few years ago, I submitted a press release to the publication. But six months later, there was no response, and the release was not published. So I called the editor to inquire about the matter. The editor apologized and said he'd meant to run the piece but he'd misplaced it and soon forgot about it. He said he would look for the material I'd sent and if he couldn't find it, he would call me.

To my utter delight, he found the release and re-worked it as a profile. He published it, along with my photo, in the very next issue of the magazine. In fact, the article can still be read today on the magazine's web site.

Stories like this are not uncommon. I've had similar experiences with book publishers, some of which have resulted in book deals. The same could happen to you when you make a "courtesy call" about your submissions.

12. You don't include photographs or you fail to mention their availability.

So what if you're not Brad Pitt or Angelina Jolie. A quality photo can increase your chances of seeing print. In fact, some stories require a good picture and they will not be run without it.

While reporting for the *The Record Herald* (Waynesboro, PA) in the '90s, I read a press release one day and saw the potential for a good story. So I called up the contact person and asked for a photo.

"Oh, no," she said. "I'm not photogenic."

"But this is a good story and my editor won't touch it without a picture."

"Well, let me talk to my husband."

"That's fine ma'am, but we'd like to run this story in tomorrow's paper."

The woman thought for a moment and said, "I need to get my hair done. Can you wait a day?"

"Not sure, but I'll mention it to my editor."

We never received the photo and the story never saw print—something that could have been avoided.

13. You place all of your eggs in one basket.

The press release is an important tool for public relations, but to rely on that tool alone would be foolhearty and costly. The same can be said of any media document. As the saying goes, "There's strength in numbers." This is particularly true where visibility and exposure are concerned. Indeed, the more resources you draw on for your campaign, the greater your chances of succeeding. All too often, however, eager businesspeople become overconfident in a single tool. This results in limited or even disappointing exposure.

If you think this "one-basket" mistake is elementary and that no business professional would do such a thing, think again. I once worked for a company that poured all of its marketing dollars into full-page ads in trade magazines. When I suggested a publicity plan that allowed for free mentions in the same publications, I was brushed aside. Determined to save the company money, I proposed a national TV strategy that would put the company on news programs and radio talk shows. Again, I was brushed aside. The company moved forward with its giant advertising plan. And the results? A major financial loss, and only a few new customers to show for the flawed campaign.

Put simply: If you'd like to maximize your public relations efforts—and get more for your money—you need an approach that integrates multiple marketing resources. Ideally, you'd use as many as you can afford. Instead of relying on a single tool or media document, important as it may be, simply expand your toolbox. Include such tools as advertisements, direct mail, public speaking, newsletters, telemarketing, etc. Resist the urge to gamble most of your budget on a single method or publicity tool.

If you'd like to maximize your public relations efforts—and get more for your money—you need an approach that integrates multiple marketing resources.

For the most part, the resources you choose will be determined by your time, budget, and the goals of your campaign. But what you can't do in the current campaign can likely be done in the next one. Consider testing different tools with each campaign. Try something different each year. Closely monitor your work and experiment to see what brings the best results.

14. You haven't learned to spin.

Everywhere you turn today, there's talk about "spin" control in the media. Typically, when a politician or government leader makes a mistake or says something that can be detrimental to a campaign, he or she issues a statement that puts a spin on the negative news. In other words, they try very hard to turn a negative into a positive.

When you can master this part of public relations, you are pretty much unstoppable in your quest for profit-building publicity. It's unfortunate, however, that some professionals have not learned this method of public relations. Some, it seems, take a passive approach to negative events while hoping for the best. If they respond to negative press coverage, they respond too late. Take Senator John Kerry for example. We all remember that during the final leg of his presidential campaign, he initially ignored the negative information that was highly publicized about the "Swift Boat" incident. After Kerry saw a huge drop in his poll numbers, he began to respond. But to his dismay, he responded too late.

Before starting your campaign, try to anticipate problems, unexpected trouble, and any type of bad case scenarios. Think of how you can turn these negatives into positives if you're ever required to do so.

15. You don't "talk it up" when it comes to your campaign.

Public speaking is a vital part of any public relations campaign. To attempt a campaign without it is like driving a car with three tires. In other words, something would be missing. Despite its importance, however, some professionals (undoubtedly introverts at heart) let shyness or fear of speaking rob them of many profit-building publicity opportunities.

"If you're like most people, public speaking is probably not your favorite activity," said copywriter Peter Fogel (*The Golden Thread*, Sept. 11, 2006). "However, it's an activity that will rapidly become one of your favorites when you let it give your career the huge boost it has given mine. The quickest way to make yourself the 'expert' … is to stand in front of a room full of eager, targeted clients who are there to gain the information and knowledge they need. And you're the one who's giving it to them."

Fogel notes that the forum for public speaking also provides a quick way to build your opt-in list for future contacts and communication. You only need to collect the names and contact information of all the people who attend your meeting.

When you give talks about your cause (or your business), you give traction to an otherwise decent campaign. When people hear of your talks, they think, "Oh, that's the woman who was featured in the paper." You may have been an "unknown" before your name and face showed up on TV, but now you're becoming quite popular. At this point, when you request a speaking engagement, the people know who you are, and they are more likely to invite you to come and dazzle their meetings.

One of my favorite books on this topic is *How to Make a Fortune from Public Speaking: Put Your Money Where Your Mouth Is* by Robert Anthony

(New York, NY: Berkley Publishing Group, 1988). This little book, which is now out of print, was the tool that got me started as a professional speaker. The author shows in unmistakable terms how to blend your work in print with simple talks, workshops, and seminars. He shows you how to use public speaking to take your publicity efforts to the next level.

16. You do not write articles or books for publication.

Take a moment and reflect on your last public relations campaign. Take a look at your clip file. How many press releases did you have published? How many articles? Was there a book or booklet published? If not, then you left money on the table.

Publishing articles is a cut above having a press release published; and publishing a book is even better. Truth be told, becoming a published author (of articles or books) is the quickest way to establish yourself as an authority in your field. When readers see your name in print, they come to see you as an expert. This enhances your credibility, widens your platform, increases your income, and enhances your image before your audience.

Thanks to the Internet, many smart marketers have found the distribution of free articles in e-zines to be an effective method for generating leads and making sales. Judy Cullins, editor of "The Book Coach Says" e-zine, practically swears by this method. Her articles appear in scores of online publications and they result in steady traffic to her site. A quick search of Judy's name on Google shows her articles are posted everywhere. One of the keys to making this work is to include a detailed "Author's Bio" at the end of the article. This section, also called "Resource Box," provides contact information and other resources for the readers.

"Although I send out my share of press releases, for my purposes, the most powerful public relations tool I've used is articles," says Beth Ann Erickson. "I whip up a new article on a regular basis and submit them to my favorite article directory. It's a totally free service (unlike many press release sites) and will get my targeted article directly in front of the audience I'm trying to attract."

17. You don't recycle or pyramid your publishing achievements.

Collecting your published press releases and articles in a clip file is commendable; but keeping them there is a mistake. Why?

Publishing articles is a cut above having a press release published; and publishing a book is even better.

No good piece of writing should die an early death. Instead, it should be picked up and re-used in as many ways as possible. For example, your press release can be recycled as a brochure or a direct mail piece. It can also hold a place on your web site.

Your published articles can become chapters in a book, or the contents of a series of talks. They can even be used in your own newsletter or placed on a CD and sold to your audience.

Since the bulk of your work was done in the initial writing process of these documents, recycling this work requires little time and effort.

18. You are neither consistent nor persistent in your publicity efforts.

Another common mistake made in publicity campaigns is the failure to maintain—the inability (for whatever reason) to keep going, even when all seems well. The issue here is the importance of frequency. Your audience must see your name and face over and over on a regular basis. Only then will they think of you first when they have a need.

Your audience must see your name and face over and over on a regular basis. Only then will they think of you first when they have a need.

"While it takes a long time to build your name recognition in the marketplace, it takes no time at all for people to forget about you," says publicist Pam Lontos. "So you have to maintain the frequency of your publicity throughout the life of your business, especially when your competition maintains the frequency of theirs. Otherwise, you become old news."

As soon as you succeed with one area of your campaign, begin immediately on another area. Contact other publications. Write a new article. Give a new speech. Run a new ad. Do what you can to keep the media wave going. This consistent practice will ensure your place above the competition.

19. You don't keep an updated list of media contacts.

Few things can be as frustrating as having your media documents returned because the person to whom you addressed them has moved on. To avoid this type of mishap, it's imperative to keep an updated list of all your media contacts.

Let's face it. Media people are just like everyone else. They move around, take on new jobs, get promoted, start families, travel and relocate to different cities. Sometimes keeping in touch with them can be a challenge in itself. Still, it's a challenge that is worthwhile. In addition to maintaining a good relationship with your contacts, you have a benefit. Their new jobs—in different locations—could result in your story being published in different publications. This means you could tap a whole new audience of readers.

In the past, if you wanted to find a good list of media contacts, you had to purchase an expensive directory or make a trip to the library. Today, you can find this same information over the Internet.

Ideally, you should update your list at least once or twice a year. Consider using it for purposes other than your PR campaign. For example, you can use it to build rapport by sending out "thank you" cards, birthday cards, holiday greetings, etc. If you have a tip for a reporter, send him or her a note. If you have an idea for a great feature story, send it along. By doing this on a regular basis, you will become a person whom the reporter will not only remember, but one who he or she will look forward to working with. Of course, this would certainly be a feather in your hat.

20. You don't practice schmoozing with reporters.

Pam Lontos believes that your most effective PR tool is your contacts with the media on a personal level. She suggests building a personal as well as business rapport with reporters and editors.

"Find out about the kids, vacations, hobbies, and so on," she advises. "Bring some of these items up whenever you talk. People like doing business with people they like. Also, maintain your business connections. Be respectful of their time. Ask if they are on a deadline. Find out their needs and get information to them promptly."

Admittedly, some people are intimidated by reporters. But they shouldn't be. One reason is that reporters need you as much as you need them.

As a veteran newsman, I have to agree with Lontos. Although some reporters will not admit it, the fact is, they enjoy being appreciated and admired. They love receiving "thank you" cards and letters. Visit any newsroom in the country and chances are you'll find that a nice "thank you" letter is the highlight of some reporter's day.

Now if you really want to be a close buddy to a reporter, become a source for news tips and ideas. Provide information, things you really know—or have heard—about people and events outside your business interests. Do this consistently and the reporter will love you for a lifetime.

The fact is, reporters enjoy being appreciated and admired. They love receiving "thank you" cards and letters.

When I was doing investigative reporting, I often had lunch (and sometimes dinner) with the people who gave me tips for big stories. These people kept me abreast of scandals, lawsuits, new businesses coming to town, as well as plants that were shutting down. Through these contacts I learned of layoffs at major companies, the intent of business developers, and various crimes that were not covered by competing newspapers. Through these relationships it became clear that we needed each other; I help them, and they help me.

21. You don't take chances.

Sometimes you have to be bold and daring, and even unorthodox in your approach, in order to get media attention. Instead of doing business as usual, you may have to step outside your conventional thinking. Doing this, I assure you, can put your campaign into higher gear.

However, some people are not risk-takers and they don't enjoy change. Consequently good opportunities may pass them by. Here's an example:

I was talking to a retailer about his marketing campaign when I learned some fascinating things about his past. He had been raised in a foster home and survived a childhood that was filled with abuse and neglect. Despite all this, he managed to finish school, married a good woman, and became a successful businessman.

"Have you considered sharing this with the paper," I asked. "It's a strong human interest story that will inspire a lot of people."

"Nope," he said. "It's too personal. Can't do that."

"At this time, your ads and press releases are being buried deep inside the paper," I explained. "But if you told this story to a reporter, you and your business could make the front page, or get a lot of space on the feature page."

He was not convinced.

"Imagine this," I said. "If the reporter published the story and then forwarded it to the Associated Press, you and your business would become known throughout the country. How about it?"

The businessman said he understood but that he wasn't ready to share that part of his life. Well, I understood his concerns, but I also understood what he missed out on by refusing to take a chance. "All life is a chance," said Dale Carnegie. "The person who goes the furthest is generally the one who is willing to do and dare."

22. You don't piggyback on current events.

Billy Graham has said that he reads most of the major newspapers each day along with his Bible. This allows him to be informed, current, and relevant in his preaching. As a result of this practice, he's able to frequently tie the day's news into his sermons. By mentioning the news that's on everybody's mind, he's able to relate to his audience while driving his message home.

The common name for this concept is "piggyback." It simply means that you promote your business by riding the wave of current events. You analyze your promotion and determine how it can tie in with the news on TV or in print. Then you write a press release with this tie-in and submit it to the press. You can also go a step farther by offering expert interviews on the subject.

After the Katrina disaster in New Orleans in 2005, many businesses began promoting survival kits. Those in the knife industry talked about the knives most suitable for disasters. Others talked about preparation of food and water. Although some may see this as exploiting a tragedy, it can be argued that these businesses were also meeting needs and helping to save lives from future disasters.

With some creative thinking, practically any product or service can be made to fit a current news story. So find out what's hot, latch on to it, and then ride it with all you've got!

This list is an overview of the most common mistakes made on the road to fame. It is offered to make you aware of possible weaknesses in your own campaign. Feel free to use this as a guide. Better yet, think of it as a check-list for troubleshooting your work whenever you need to contact the press. Since the path to media coverage is fraught with challenges, the more you know about what to do—and what *not* to do—the better your chances of being covered.

With some creative thinking, practically any product or service can be made to fit a current news story.

Chapter 2

The 13 Essential Tools for Launching an Effective Publicity Campaign

What You Need to Become "Newsworthy" and Exploit the Media

IN AN ARTICLE ENTITLED, "HAVING THE RIGHT TOOLS MAKES FIGHTING THE Fall Leaf War a Breeze," reporter Mike Ferrara writes about the seasonal challenges of homeowners.

"It's fall. That means it is time to haul out all of the weapons for the annual war on leaves," he begins. "For lazy homeowners like me, that means bringing in the big guns—the tools and technology that make the task as easy as possible."

After describing a few of his favorite tools, he closes his piece with this comment: "Whether the approach is high-tech or traditional, choosing the right lawn tools can help get the job done quicker."

These comments about tools for the lawn provide a good lesson for people in business, especially those planning a PR campaign. The bottom line is: Having the right tools for the task at hand can make all the difference. And, I should add, knowing how to use these tools will determine your level of success.

Admittedly, campaigns of any nature are hard work. They are demanding and trying. They can be costly, stressful, and even disappointing, to say the least. They can even bring out the worst in people. Yet, by having the right tools and knowing how to use them, the job is much easier.

Following is a list of the most important tools you'll need for a successful publicity campaign. Most will not be needed every campaign or for all aspects of a single campaign. Still, having each of them at your disposal will make you better prepared for your campaign experience. If nothing else, they will make you more media savvy than some of your competition.

13 Essential Tools for Your Promotional Campaign

Because publicity is primarily about generating coverage by the news media, a number of these tools are used for communicating directly with editors, reporters, and producers. Take a moment to review them and determine how they can work in your campaign. Who knows, you may be pleasantly surprised.

1. Slogan or tag line

In an interview with Jay Leno, shock jock Howard Stern said something that is quite important for business professionals. He said he learned that Michael Jackson was the first who called himself, "The King of Pop." Later, the media and everyone else began calling him by that title. Howard's reaction? "So I began calling myself 'The King of All Media.'" Now everyone refers to Howard by that title.

Since perception is often reality for many people, it pays to have a slogan that positions you or your business in the marketplace.

Since perception is often reality for many people, it pays to have a slogan that positions you or your business in the marketplace. Think of your ultimate goal and what you would like to be called. How would you like to be known? Once you arrive at a decision, create a slogan that drives your message home.

Every business needs a slogan, a tag line that states its purpose and sets it apart from the competition. It should state your Unique Selling Proposition (USP) in a snap. According to Dan S. Kennedy, author of *The Ultimate Marketing Plan* (Holbrook, MA: Adams Media Corp., 2000), your unique sales message or slogan is "a way of summarizing and telegraphing one of the chief benefits or the chief benefit of the business, product, or service being marketed."

When Wal-Mart labels itself with "Always Low Prices," it has made a positioning promise and stated its position against the competition. Wal-Mart's slogan is repeated so often that the average consumer knows it by heart.

You can follow Wal-Mart's example. Once you have created a slogan for your business, it should be featured in all of your media documents and in all aspects of your public relations campaign. When you're asked to give a talk, ask to be introduced with your slogan. When you write a letter, include your slogan. You can also add it to your answering machine and the signature line of your e-mail. Do this long enough and the media, as well as your audience, will begin using your slogan. Then when your name is ever mentioned, people will quickly associate you with your slogan, just like Michael Jackson and Howard Stern. More will be shared on this in the next chapter.

2. Mailing lists

Having a good mailing list is like having money on hold: You can draw on it anytime you have a need.

*H*aving a good
mailing list is
like having
money on hold:
You can draw on
it anytime you
have a need.

As part of a campaign, your mailing lists should target three groups:

- **The media:** Keep an updated list of names of editors, reporters, producers, and talk shows (TV and radio). This list is a must for generating press coverage. Remember to target the media that fits your news. Do not use the shotgun approach. This is very critical when contacting trade publications, most of which serve a specific niche.

- **Prospects:** You may choose from any number of reliable list brokers and companies. You can rent thousands of names within specific demographics. You can locate prospects on a local, regional, or national level.

- **Clients/Customers:** Your own in-house list is the most valuable for lead generation and direct sales. Since you don't have to rent the names from an outside source, the savings are quite noticeable when you promote via direct mail.

3. Press release

The single most important element in a public relations campaign is the press release. It is absolutely essential for making contact with the media. When combined with a hefty press kit, it provides you a powerful arsenal for dramatically improving your campaign.

A key reason the press release is so essential is that it helps both you and the press. You have the benefit of coverage and the press has the benefit of filling its pages or news segments. In his book, *The Copywriter's Handbook* (New York, NY: Henry Holt and Co., 2005), Robert W. Bly cites a study by the *Columbia Journalism Review* in which it surveyed an issue of *The Wall Street Journal* to determine the number of stories generated by press releases. The study found that 111 stories on the inside pages were taken from press releases, either word for word or paraphrased.

A press release is all about news. It's a simple one- or two-page document that features news about you or your business. It carries a headline and is written in the style of a news story. All important information is mentioned in the first two paragraphs. And as its name implies, it is released to the press.

It should be noted, however, that the publication of a press release is at the discretion of the editor, who may run it as is (with minor changes) or use it to develop a full-length story or article. Here's a sample of a press release prepared by professional trainer Alan Lane of Lane Training Solutions:

Contact: Alan Lane

FOR IMMEDIATE RELEASE

Company: Lane Training Solutions
Address: 506 C Lynnehaven Drive
Hagerstown, MD 21742
Phone: (800) 000-0000
E-mail: Alan@lanesolutions.net
Web site: www.lanesolutions.net

Date: Sept. 6, 2006

ALAN LANE NAMED COLUMNIST FOR BUSINESS NEWSMAGAZINE

Column offers monthly tips on marketing, sales and customer service

WILLISTON, S.C.—A native of Williston has been tapped to write a monthly column for a Washington, DC-based business newsmagazine.

Alan Lane will be published by The Tidal Wave Business Newsmagazine, a publication that covers the business community of Washington and Baltimore, MD.

The column is called "Tidal Wave Marketing 101." It offers practical tips for customer service, marketing, sales and professional training for businesses. Lane, a professional trainer and consultant, views the column as an extension of his consulting services.

"I am thrilled to be able to help others achieve their goals by providing insight and techniques to improve customer relations," Lane said.

Lane is director of Lane Training Solutions, a consulting and training company that teaches businesses how to improve customer relations. His work has also been featured in Publishers' Auxiliary, the official publication of the National Newspaper Association.

For more information, visit www.lanesolutions.net or call _____

—End—

A press release should be submitted to the press whenever you have news to report. Otherwise, plan on releasing them on a monthly or bimonthly basis during your campaign. Ideally, you should use them routinely as a usual part of your business, with or without a major campaign.

4. Press kit

The press kit is an intrinsic element of any public relations effort and isn't relegated only to literary campaigns.

"A press kit is to publicity what thunder is to lightning. Without it, a campaign has no voice." This is what Jodee Blanco says in *The Complete Guide to Book Publicity* (New York, NY: Allworth Press, 2000). Going further, she writes, "The press kit is an intrinsic element of any public relations effort and isn't relegated only to literary campaigns."

Indeed, a press kit is the foundation of any media relations program. In the simplest terms, the press kit is a folder with two-sided pockets that contains numerous media documents about you and your company. These documents may include:

▶ Press release
▶ Bio sheet
▶ Company history
▶ Fact sheet
▶ Brochure
▶ Press clips about you or your business
▶ Clips of published articles
▶ Testimonials
▶ Photos
▶ Any other items that are relevant to your story.

For instance, you could also include a book, tape, or CD of one of your television interviews. What you include will depend on your targeted media and what you want to accomplish.

The information in a press kit is organized in a reader-friendly manner and designed to entice reporters and editors into doing a story about your company. These documents should prove you are worthy of news coverage.

At the same time, they should make the reporter's job easy by answering their questions. "When a press kit, or press packet, is used properly," says Thomas Bivins, "it can effectively aid in message dissemination by adding the right amount of unduplicated information to the media mix."

Given the popularity of the Internet, it is now common, and even required in some cases, to have your press kit posted on a web site. This saves you money—and the reporter, time—when he or she needs information in a hurry.

5. Internet communications

OK. This is a no-brainer as no sensible businessperson can ignore the marketing and promotional opportunities provided by Internet technology. No one can deny the ease of use, the money you save, and the targeted audience you can reach by tapping this technology.

No sensible businessperson can ignore the marketing and promotional opportunities provided by Internet technology.

Perhaps you already have a web site and you're using it to the best of your ability. But keep in mind all of the other ways you can promote online. A few of them include the use of e-mail campaigns (without spamming), e-mail courses about your product or services, fax blasts, e-newsletters, discussion groups, and blogs. Don't forget the power of webcasts, webcams, webinars and web affiliate programs.

When I check my e-mail each day, I'm often snowed under with e-zines. Most of the publishers frequently promote online courses, e-books, teleseminars, and webinars. Sometimes the offerings appear endless. My schedule would never allow me to participate in all of the seminars and discussions, but I take note of what's being offered. This way, I can keep abreast of the tools being used.

To get a sense of how these Internet tools are applied, sign up for a few e-zines that deal with the topic of your business. Take a few online courses and participate in web seminars. Look in on discussion groups and ask questions. Pay attention to the marketers who appear to be most successful. After you have made a few notes, study ways you can use this technology in your campaign.

6. Newsletter

The newsletter remains one of the most effective tools available for creating goodwill and promoting your business on a personal, professional, and ongoing basis. Today, many writers and entrepreneurs use online newsletters to reach out to their audience on a regular basis. This is no surprise when you consider the low cost and ease-of-work involved in publishing a newsletter.

Of course, there are many reasons a newsletter should be used in a promotional campaign.

- ▶ It can be any size and follow any design.
- ▶ It can be a simple two-paged job with text on the front and back of a single sheet of paper, or a four-pager with typewritten text.
- ▶ It can be full of color and sport fancy graphics and typeface.
- ▶ It can use photos and cartoons, or text only.
- ▶ It can be published weekly, biweekly, monthly, quarterly, or as often as you like. After all, you're the publisher, so you're in control.
- ▶ If money is an issue, you can go the online route. Create an e-zine to bypass the cost of printing and postage.

Your newsletter can be used for any number of purposes. In addition to telling customers, clients, and prospects about your new products and services, you can promote speaking engagements, seminars, special offers, news, and even personal tidbits about you and your family. Beyond these factors, a good newsletter will keep you visible before your audience. At the same time, it will enable you to build rapport with readers, as well as customer loyalty, while positioning yourself as a leader in your field.

A good newsletter will enable you to build rapport with readers, as well as customer loyalty, while positioning yourself as a leader in your field.

Another key benefit of the newsletter is that it can actually make money. This is done through subscription sales and by selling ad space. In most cases, subscriptions are sold when you offer specialized information to a niche market.

In terms of selling ads and other products with online publications, Angela Adair-Hoy, publisher of WritersWeekly.com, is a big believer who has found much success in this area. In her book, *Profitable Email Publishing* (Bangor, ME: Deep South Publishing Co./Booklocker.com, 2001), she writes: "Using your computer and modem, you can attract thousands of subscribers (customers) and collect hundreds or even thousands per month from advertisers while selling your own products and services!"

As with your other media documents, a newsletter can be mailed to customers, clients, prospects, schools, and yes, the press.

When designing your newsletter, use a catchy title that reflects your business. Use a tag line that reinforces your sales message. Include your photo in every issue. (More will be said about this later.)

7. Brochure or flier

"Not everyone has a budget for media advertising, but almost every business needs and produces promotional material," say advertising experts Kenneth Roman and Jane Maas. "Some brochures are clearly more effective than others, attracting more attention, inviting readers, and increasing sales. Others are a waste of time and production money."

I think it is safe to say that no public relations campaign is complete without a good brochure. These handy documents, sometimes called "folders," "slim jims," and "broadsides," are ideal for telling a complete story about your business, your products, or services. Done right, they will be saved by your audience or passed along, like gospel tracts.

I think it is safe to say that no public relations campaign is complete without a good brochure.

Brochures are sort of Herculean among public relations tools. Why? They can be used in any forum and for any purpose. They can be plain or full of color; or they can be small or large and possess only a few pages or many pages.

Brochures can be served as standalone tools on a rack, like you see in a doctor's office. They can be placed on counters near cash registers. They can be handed out at trade shows or placed on chairs at speaking engagements. You can also use them in your direct mail package or include them with your press releases (or press kits). These documents can also be formatted for your web site.

The uses of brochures are many. For instance, you can use them to provide solid how-to information about your product or service. You can use them as tip sheets, or to tell the history of your company. You can also use them to explain how your products and services work, or as a forum for Frequently Asked Questions. They can be used as mini-catalogs and even include coupons. They can be used to reinforce a fundraising message. Or they can be used to promote a political message that sets you apart from your opponents.

Where sales are concerned, brochures must have all the elements of a good advertisement: Strong headlines on the cover and at the top of each page, highlighted benefits, features, testimonials, a call to action, and a response device.

8. Articles

"The fastest way to build your name and become famous is to get PUB-LISHED," says Dr. Robert Anthony in *How to Make a Fortune from Public Speaking* (New York, NY: Berkley Books, 1983).

I have found Anthony's statement to be true in my own case as well as the cases of my clients and many other business professionals. Getting published provides instant name recognition and it can lead not only to good public relations, but to speaking engagements, interviews (TV and print), and added income.

If you want to use this effective PR tool (and I suggest you do), you don't have to start by writing a book. Begin with an article.

The type of article you could write is limited only by your imagination. Profiles, how-to, self-help, features, investigative, historical, new product, human interest, and religious articles all are needed by newspapers and magazines. Whichever type you choose, just remember to keep your slogan—your unique sales message—in mind. If you can't weave this message into your article, be sure to include it in your bio section at the end of the piece.

Profiles, how-to, self-help, features, investigative, historical, new product, human interest, and religious articles all are needed by newspapers and magazines.

One of the great benefits of an article is that it's ideal for recycling. You can turn it into a Special Report or White Paper, and then sell it directly or offer it as premium incentive. A single article can be used as a speech or the content for a workshop; a series of articles can be transformed into a book. All this means you will also tap a larger audience, and thereby strengthen your publicity campaign.

So you see that writing articles will add tremendously to your campaign. But how do you get published?

Start by writing a query letter to the editor of the publication in which you want to be published. This is a single-page sales letter that pitches your idea. Give a working title and explain how it meets the needs of the editor's readers. Give the estimated length and note whether photos will be included. State your credentials and ask if you may submit the article. You could note that your published clips (providing you are published) are available on request.

Be prepared for rejection. If it occurs, simply send the query to another magazine. Remember, persistence pays.

9. Speeches

It's been said that there are two times in your life when you are totally alone: When you die, and just before you give a speech. This may well be true. But the fact is public speaking is well worth the stress and all the fear that comes along with it. In public relations, as well as publicity in particular, public speaking is an essential tool for putting a face and voice on your efforts. It's also a powerful way to move audiences and cement your sales message into their thinking.

"The opportunities that await you as a professional speaker are tremendous," says Dr. Robert Anthony. "Admittedly, taking the first step is the most difficult of all. But once you've started, each step will get easier and easier."

The type of speeches you give will depend on your audience and the aim of your campaign. You can target schools, churches, seminars and workshops, conferences, business luncheons, libraries, political gatherings, etc. In *Handbook for Public Relations Writing* (Lincolnwood, IL: NTC Business Books, 1989), Thomas Bivins outlines three purposes:

- ▶ **Speeches to inform:** The purpose is to define, clarify, instruct, or demonstrate.

- ▶ **Speeches to persuade:** The purpose is to convince or influence and often carries a call to action.

- ▶ **Speeches to entertain:** The purpose is broad and intended for celebration, eulogies, and dinner engagements.

There's also the "elevator speech." It's a quick, 30-second talk designed to tell a person (or group) about your business in the fewest words possible. Along with this, I'd add the all-important "sound bite." No, it's not a speech, per se, but it's something that all good speakers must master. In short, it's a catchy, memorable phrase that you throw out to reporters during an interview. They work like magic when done on TV or radio. Sound bites should be repeated throughout your campaign.

10. Books and booklets

Marketing expert Joe Vitale had always been a popular speaker, but when he wrote, *The AMA's Guide to Small Business Advertising* for the American Marketing Association, his number of clients and speaking engagements went through the roof. He recalls, "I knew about advertising before I wrote the book. But they didn't call on me then. Now that I've written this book, people call me all the time to come and speak about advertising. Why? Because they now view me as an authority. The book is what made the difference."

A published book can make a huge difference in your public relations campaign.

A published book can also make a huge difference in your public relations campaign. When beginning, choose a topic that ties in perfectly with your business. It can be how-to or self-help, or even biographical if you have a compelling story.

Once you've decided on the type of book you want to write, write a catchy title and subtitle, both of which should reflect your slogan or sales message. Draw up a chapter-by-chapter outline of the book and begin writing. Aim for 100 to 200 pages. If you cannot write it because of time or the lack of talent, don't worry. You can hire a ghostwriter, local reporter, or English major at the local college.

When the manuscript is complete, you're ready to contact book editors via a query and then a proposal. The query is the pitch letter for the book idea; the proposal consists of a summary of the book, its market, your qualifications, the competition, outline, and sample chapters. Depending on the nature of the book, you may require a literary agent to get your foot in the door. Otherwise, you can contact smaller publishers.

Unless you go the self-publishing route, getting a book published in time for a campaign is next to impossible. If the work of writing, editing, printing, binding, and distributing a full-length book doesn't appeal to you, then settle (at least for now) on releasing a booklet.

"When you undertake a subscription newsletter you have necessarily bound yourself to producing a product at regular and announced intervals," says Dr. Jeffery Lant in *No More Cold Calls* (Cambridge, MA: JLA Publications, 1993). "This is not the case with booklets and books, which is why perhaps, I prefer them."

Lant has single-handedly made millions of dollars from his books alone. All of them were self-published and marketed to the business industry. He offers the following reasons for publishing booklets:

I often tell marketers to take a lesson from the televangelists, most of whom publish booklets that include full pages of ad copy about their respective ministries.

▶ **Permanence:** People will toss aside a brochure or postcard, but they are less likely to throw away a booklet. By keeping the booklet, they are keeping your unique sales message that's printed inside.

▶ **Rapport:** People spend time with you by reading your booklet. They feel this tool allows them the privilege of getting to know you.

▶ **Distribution:** Books and booklets can be distributed in schools, stores, libraries, and other channels. If your competition is not an author, he or she does not have publications available through these channels.

I often tell marketers to take a lesson from the televangelists, most of whom publish booklets that include full pages of ad copy about their respective ministries.

If you wonder about the value of booklets to your campaign, take a look at the booklet queen, Paulette Ensign of Tips Products International. Some years ago she self-published a booklet entitled, *110 Ideas for Organizing Your Business Life*. She priced the 16-pager at $5 a copy. To promote it, she began sending letters and copies of the booklet to targeted media outlets. In a very short time, she'd sold thousands of copies and was flooded with invitations to give talks and workshops. Ensign eventually sold over a million copies of the booklet.

"Booklets are merely elaborated special reports," says Dr. Jeffrey Lant. "Ten printed pages is a good minimum length for a booklet. That's surely possible for you. This constitutes both a good learning experience and, again, a good premium ... and profit center."

11. Column

When I wanted to enhance my reputation as an authority on community journalism, I began writing a monthly column for *Publishers' Auxiliary*, the official publication of the National Newspaper Association. After my third article appeared, I began receiving requests to do workshops for various state press associations.

When I wanted to make a name for myself as a copywriter for the non-profits, I began writing a column for *Fund Raising Management* magazine, a publication of Hoke Communications Inc. By the time my second article appeared, I had picked up a national client.

These experiences illustrate the possibilities you have by writing a column. It doesn't matter whether it appears in the local newspaper, a trade journal, or an e-zine. A column will give you credibility and catapult you before a wider audience. Not only will you be known by a growing number of readers, but your promotions will be ever before them.

And since you will be viewed as an expert, you will be called upon to speak, to give workshops.

Other benefits include payment for the column. That's right. You could be paid a fee by the newspaper or magazine, or you may self-syndicate the column to other publications. If you're lucky, you can sell it to a national syndicate.

You can also recycle your column by compiling the work into a book. I've done this with a number of my books. For example, *The Better Letter: Essential Tips for Effective Fundraising Copy* (Target Marketing Group/ NAPCO, 2006) is basically a compilation of my columns from Fund Raising Management. Thanks to my publisher, that column is seeing new life—and reaching new readers. The same could happen to you.

After my third article appeared, I began receiving requests to do workshops for various state press associations.

In addition to all of the above benefits, writing a column gives you a new title: "Columnist." This alone carries a certain degree of prestige. So don't shy away from using it. After all, it suggests that you are not only a published writer, but that your work is recognized by the media. This is legitimate credibility without any hype.

When you're introduced as a speaker, the audience can be told, "Mrs. Jane Doe is a columnist for ...." Or, "Mr. John Doe writes a monthly column on ...."

Having this title will also open doors to the media, especially trade publications. When they see that you write professionally—and that you can make deadlines—they are more inclined to read your queries and take a look at your articles—or book manuscript. If you're fortunate, as I was in one case, an editor will ask if she can also run your column in her publication.

As with other tools mentioned here, the type of column you write will be determined by the goals of your campaign and the image you want to project. Luckily, you have a number of formats from which to choose. You can use how-to, question and answer, advice (like Ann Landers), public service (for nonprofits), historical, opinion, political, commentary, or anything pertaining to your industry.

Be sure to include your photo and a detailed Resource Box at the end of each section. The Resource Box (a term coined by Dr. Jeffrey Lant) is the "About the Author" section that describes who you are. It includes your product or service, and contact information.

12. Direct mail

In his delightful book on direct marketing, Richard V. Benson made an interesting comment about selling by mail: "I know of no better way to make money and have fun than being in direct mail."

This is not surprising when you consider the many advantages of this powerful tool. Among other things, direct mail allows you to speak directly to your audience on a one-on-one level. It allows you to bypass the high cost of advertising in the media. It also provides you with all the space you need to tell your story. Even more, it can support all of your PR efforts by reinforcing your slogan—your unique sales message.

Whether you want to sell directly, generate leads, or simply make your audience aware of a certain issue, direct mail is an effective way to get the job done.

Among other things, direct mail allows you to speak directly to your audience on a one-on-one level.

The classic direct mail package consists of an envelope (with a teaser on the outside), a sales letter, a flier, and an order form. A lift note (an extra item in the package that might say something like "Please read this only if you've decided not to order ...") can also be included. If you want to alert your audience to your press coverage, you can include press clips in the package. Some marketers have been known to include press releases—the same ones submitted to the media.

This promotional method also works with the media. This usually comes in the form of a pitch letter in which you ask the editor or reporter (or producer) for coverage. You explain the news angle and provide information on your background, including important dates and times. You close the letter by letting her know you are available for an interview or to simply answer questions about the topic. Such a letter can include a press release if it's pertinent.

Direct mail, in one form or another, should be a standard part of any campaign. However you use it is up to you. But do your research and try it. I think you'll be glad you did.

13. Testimonials

One sure-fire way to enhance your credibility in the eyes of the public (or your targeted audience) is to saturate your promotion with a string of powerful testimonials. You can gather them from experts, celebrities, or satisfied clients and customers. "In every field there are people whose opinion others value," says Gordon Burgett, author of *Self-Publishing to Tightly-Targeted Markets* (Santa Maria, CA: Communication Unlimited, 1989). Because of this, he says, their words, in the form of testimonials, should be placed in your books, (perhaps on the back cover) and in your flyer. Of course, this is not limited to published books; it applies to any product or service.

Start collecting testimonials early in your campaign. Then sprinkle them throughout your media documents, including press releases, direct mail, advertisements, brochures, web sites, books, and videos.

"When you can't demonstrate a product advantage, consumers have to take your word for it," say Kenneth Roman and Jane Mass in *How to Advertise* (New York, NY: St. Martin's Griffin, 1992). "They might rather take the word of fellow consumers who testify that in their experience, the product does what you say it will do."

Testimonials work because they serve as a third-party endorsement. They say to the readers (or listeners): "This is the truth." The most convincing

*T*estimonials work because they serve as a third-party endorsement. They say to the readers (or listeners): "This is the truth."

words, however, are not necessarily those of a celebrity. Instead, they are the words of a person who has actually used your product or service.

A Lesson from Harry Houdini

As we bring this section to a close, I'm reminded of the Great Harry Houdini. "He was not the best magician," said David Copperfield. "He was the best marketer."

Unlike many of his contemporary magicians, Houdini used every available tool he could find in order to promote his name and his talent. He went beyond the newspapers. He used film, books, pamphlets, speeches, and public demonstrations. He often made public challenges. In the face of competition, he redefined his magic—and his marketing—by performing more difficult stunts.

Now, many decades after his passing, we don't remember most of his competitors. But we remember him. Why? Because of his passion and the tools he used to drive his publicity campaigns.

Chapter 3

11 Tips for Crafting a Slogan or Unique Sales Message for Your Business

How to Cement Your Name or Your Sales Message into the Minds of Your Audience

D O PEOPLE WONDER ABOUT YOUR BUSINESS? DO THEY NEED A SEC-ond look at your letters or business cards to understand your purpose? Must they read pages and pages of material? Or can they tell by a mere glance at your slogan?

Since we live in an age of quick reading and short attention spans, it behooves us as business professionals to act fast in stating our purpose. Once this is revealed in a lively, succinct manner, we can get down to business. One way we can accomplish this is by using a good slogan based on the ideas of Rosser Reeves, a successful adman and the respected author of *Reality in Advertising*.

Many years ago, Reeves introduced a powerful concept for the business community known as the "Unique Selling Proposition" or "USP." The concept is basically a way to position yourself so you stand out from your competition. If your product or service is not different from or better than that of your competition, there is no reason for prospects to respond to your appeals.

Reeves stressed that in order for you to stand out, your product or service must have a USP—a major benefit that other products in its category do not offer.

Now, as a believer that marketing and fundraising are close cousins— and often live and thrive by similar rules of engagement—I believe Reeves' USP idea is also an effective concept for nonprofit groups.

A USP requires the stressing of a benefit that is unique to a particular product or service. It also must be important to the consumer. Likewise a slogan, which should be unique to a particular audience, should stress the mission of the business. And like a USP, it should be important to prospects and customers.

Why You Need a Slogan

Working with-out a slogan is like going undercover. It is moving about without an "ID tag."

No doubt about it. Every business needs a slogan. And once one has been devised, it should be "shouted from the housetops," and appear repeatedly in all forms of communications. A measure of success might be found without it, but at what cost?

Working without a slogan is like going undercover. It is moving about without an "ID tag." You might get the job done, to some degree, but only a small number of people will know you—and seek you out for help. The lack of a slogan means extra work for your mailings. You have to do more explaining about who you are and what you're doing.

On the other hand, the time spent explaining your identity could be better spent listing benefits and making the sale. In other words, if you have a good slogan—and use it lavishly—you'll be in a better position to go straight to the point.

What Is a Good Slogan?

A good slogan has certain qualities that make it work. These qualities make it memorable and lasting. Consider:

1. It is clear and concise.

It is specific and to the point, covering all the bases that need to be covered in as few words as possible. As an example, consider this well-written slogan describing Mobius, an organization in Massachusetts. It is known as "An artist-run center for experimental work in all media." The name "Mobius" may not tell you much, but the slogan sure does.

2. It sets apart your organization from others.

A church could announce that it is "a place where people are loved." But that slogan is too general and doesn't say much. The same thing can be said of many other churches. To stand out from the others, a church may pick a specialty or a certain group not highlighted by the "competition." Then something like this could be written: "We're a place where the poor are welcome." Or, "We're the place where ALL races are loved." One more: "We're the place where everyone's treated as equals."

3. It is written in the present tense.

Generally speaking, a slogan in the present tense stresses what you are doing *now* for a particular cause or business. The present tense suggests action. It implies movement, effort. It places readers in the front seats of the show. At the same time, it beckons them to come aboard and join.

A slogan in the present tense stresses what you are doing now for a particular cause or business.

4. It addresses a felt need.

What needs are you trying to meet? What help are you offering? Determine these factors. Then stress them in your slogan. For instance, if you're helping teenage mothers, you could describe your group as the place "where lonely teenage mothers find hope." Or, you could say you're "giving teenage mothers a second chance at life." Whatever you choose, the more specific, the better.

Here's a nice one I saw recently from Shiloh Christian Children's Ranch: "A Christian Refuge for Abused/Neglected Children." It doesn't use a strong action verb in the present tense, but it is loaded with specifics and heart-moving adjectives. It addresses a heart-felt need in a very clear and concise manner. When you see the slogan, you have no doubts about the focus of the organization.

5. It appeals to the people you're trying to reach.

It goes without saying that appeals should be made to people with a connection to your mission—people who have common ground with your focus. It also helps, in some cases, to include the word "You" or "Your" in the slogan.

Examples: "Helping you make a difference in your community," "Helping you honor your fallen friends," or "Helping you give the gift of life."

Where to start in choosing a winner. To create a good slogan, you may have to start thinking of it in a new light.

First and foremost, you should hone in on your purpose. You can do that by reviewing your Mission Statement. As you are well aware, your Mission Statement, formal though it is, is nothing less than a compass that keeps you on course. It is the one thing that shows you your destination. At the same time, it helps you to remain focused.

Second, look at your history. What is your success? Your strong suit? What kind of people have you helped? Who are your customers, clients, and prospects? You may have drafted a Mission Statement, but circumstances over the years may have forced you to revise it. For this reason, a new slogan is in order.

Third, consider your future. What do you expect to be doing in five years? What about ten years? These questions are crucial because a slogan needs time to catch on with prospects. And if you intend to change your focus or your mission, you may have to change your slogan as well.

6. Consider the title and subtitle of a book.

When it's time to begin writing, think of the name of your company as the title of a book and your slogan as the subtitle. One writer calls the title "The Grabber," and the subtitle, "The Descriptor."

The name of your company should grab the attention of your prospects and the slogan should describe what the "title" is all about.

In other words, the name of your company should *grab* the attention of your prospects and the slogan should *describe* what the "title" is all about.

I like to view the slogan as a backup punch (pardon the analogy): If the first one (the title/name) doesn't get you, the second one (the slogan) will.

The same principle works with newsletters, where you have a catchy title as the banner and a slogan right underneath.

7. Brainstorm.

With your Mission Statement and history in front of you, think of all the benefits you have to offer. Think of all the good you have done. Think of all the people you are reaching. Write that information down. It can be as long as a paragraph, or even a page.

8. Start cutting.

Begin cutting out all unnecessary words and phrases. Try to cut it down to a paragraph. Then a sentence. If you cannot state your purpose in a sentence, you need more cutting. The inability to summarize your work in a single sentence also may suggest your purpose is not very clear to you.

9. Rewrite the slogan.

The essence of good writing is rewriting. So don't fret if you have to sweat at it. Once you have decided on a slogan or two, put it aside for a few days. Then look at it with fresh eyes.

10. Test it orally.

Pretend you are being interviewed by a reporter and you need a single sound bite to describe your organization. How would your slogan sound if carried over the airwaves? Does it consist of too many "s's"? Is it crippled by tongue-twisters?

Pretend you're at a party and someone asks, "What is your organization?" How would your slogan sound as a response? If a saying works in speaking, there's a good chance it will work in print.

11. Test it on others.

Pass the idea around to others in your organization. You could also run it by a few newspaper editors for critique. Seek out critics who won't hesitate to disagree with you. Be hard on yourself.

In closing, let me emphasize the need for patience in developing your slogan. An author I know wrote over 100 titles during a brainstorm session for one of his books. After some time, he finally chose a winning title—and subtitle—that were instrumental in making his book a bestseller. You can do the same in selecting a winning slogan that "sells" your business.

Once you have decided on a slogan or two, put it aside for a few days. Then look at it with fresh eyes.

Chapter 4

10 Things You Should Know About Press Kits

The Elements, Design, and Use of Media Documents

YOU CAN'T FOOL THE PRESS WITH ADVERTISEMENTS DISGUISED AS news; but you can learn to court the press by making their job easier. And one way to do this is by giving reporters everything they need to do their jobs better.

Perhaps no other promotional tool accomplishes this better than the standard press kit. This package of information (often called "information kit," "publicity kit," and "media kit") may be used for a broad variety of PR purposes. Usually it is handed out at product promotion presentations or press conferences. It is not advisable, or necessary, to send out a press kit every time you contact a reporter. In most cases, a press release will do just fine. But for special occasions, and when you have news that is significantly important, a press kit is recommended.

Even though the press kit may serve many purposes, the key to assembling one is to keep in mind the needs of those receiving it. At the very least, the press kit should include:

- ▶ **A cover letter:** This is optional.
- ▶ **A table of contents:** This depends on the number of documents included.
- ▶ **A press release:** This is the most important item.
- ▶ **Photo:** This could be a professional picture of you or your staff.
- ▶ **A bio sheet:** This is like a modified resume.
- ▶ **A backgrounder or fact sheet:** As the name implies, it provides the history of your company.
- ▶ **A brochure or flier:** This reinforces the message in your letter and press release.
- ▶ **Clips:** These consist of published articles and news stories about you or your company.
- ▶ **Annual report:** This is used only if relevant to the campaign.

Other items may include books (or booklets), newsletters, video and CDs, or anything else that will add to the news angle of your campaign. These promotional items are usually placed in a plain or colorful folder (with pockets). Your name, company, logo, or even a photo, may be placed on the front cover of the folder. A business card is usually attached inside.

OK. So now you know the basics of assembling a press kit. Let's see how you can use your kit to please editors and generate coverage.

1. It should always include a press release.

No press kit is complete without a press release. While it may or may not include a cover letter and other promotional documents, it would be a mistake to omit the press release.

As a reporter, I always looked first at the press release whenever I received a press kit. It didn't matter who sent it and I didn't care about the size of the company. I wanted to know one thing: What's the news angle?

As far as I was concerned, the press release was the centerpiece that told me what I needed to know. Everything else was supportive.

While it may or may not include a cover letter and other promotional documents, it would be a mistake to omit the press release.

2. It should always include a photograph.

When using a photograph, be sure to use one that's taken by a professional, and not an amateur using the latest cell phone technology. Remember, your press kit is your way of selling yourself as a true professional. So everything, especially the photograph, should portray you in the best light. "Not only is it important to have a high quality photograph," says Elane Feldman in *Self-*

Promotion and Publicity for Authors, "you want one that presents you in the best light—literally and figuratively."

Editors, reporters, and producers welcome good photographs. They know their value. They understand that photos can allow you to put a face on a problem or a solution. And faces, mind you, can be more memorable than words.

The type of photo you use will depend on the purpose of your campaign. However, every business professional should have available a clean head-and-shoulders portrait.

After having your photo taken, the next step is to identify the person (or persons) in the picture. If a caption is required, then attach it to the photo.

3. It should be a unified package with each piece projecting your image and purpose.

Everything in your package should reflect your sales message (or slogan) and the image you want to project.

Everything in your package should reflect your sales message (or slogan) and the image you want to project. If your press release is about one thing, and your brochures and clips are about another, then something is missing. Remember, your goal is to make the editor's job easier. And one way to do this is by making your package well organized and easy to follow.

4. It can be of any size.

Clients will sometimes ask me about the size of the press kit and whether it is possible to have too many documents. My answer is simple: It depends. It depends on the story you want covered and it depends on the media you want to cover it. Let me explain.

If you have a complicated story that's not easily understood, then it's OK to make your package larger than usual. If you're contacting a national news organization and you need to impress them by proving you're worthy of national attention, then a larger-than-usual press kit is fine. I would also encourage the use of a larger press kit if your news is highly controversial.

On the other hand, if you're contacting your local newspaper, or regional trade publication, a smaller press kit would be more appropriate. Keep in mind, if a reporter needs more information, he or she will call you. In general, my rule of thumb is: the bigger the media, the bigger the press kit; the smaller the media, the smaller the press kit. When in doubt, include the extra documents.

5. It should accommodate changes and breaking news.

A good press kit is not static, but evolving. It is flexible and often changes with the news. Your campaign may have started with a central news angle, but along the way, you reached certain goals and made other achievements. When this happens, it's time to create new documents that reflect the latest news and make them a part of your press package.

"A smart publicist knows that the press kit, just like the campaign itself, needs to grow and evolve with each moment-to-moment accomplishment," says publicist Jodee Blanco. "As a publicist, you have to stay on your toes, monitoring print and broadcast coverage."

6. It is great for pyramiding your press clips.

Your press kit may have started out with only one or two clippings. But as you move forward and generate interest in your campaign, you'll soon have other clips to add to the package.

Each time you get a "hit" (something published) simply add it to the kit. If you write an article and have it published, you can add it to the kit. As your media package grows with the addition of these new clips, you become more and more newsworthy in the eyes of the press.

As your media package grows with the addition of these new clips, you become more and more newsworthy in the eyes of the press.

7. It is suitable for print and online distribution.

I am always surprised to learn of businesspeople who have forsaken print and insist on putting all of their press documents on a web site. They forget that large numbers of people, including the press, still enjoy receiving mail the old-fashioned way. Many (myself included), prefer printed documents over the Internet any day of the week.

Therefore, to ensure your chances of success, design your press kit for both audiences—print and online readers. Do not become so caught up with the latest technology that you wind up excluding parts of your audience.

8. It should always be ready for instant distribution.

Whatever stage your business or campaign is in, you can benefit tremendously from having a basic press kit on hand—and ready to release in a moment's notice. "Even if you don't plan to launch a promotional campaign anytime in the near future," say the authors of *Getting Business to Come to You*, "we advise putting together the components for a publicity kit now and maintaining it, because you never know when publicity will tap you on the shoulder unexpectedly; and when it does, you'll want to be ready to respond."

9. It should fit the media.

When mailing your press kit to a television producer, it is common practice to include a video recording of your speaking or of you being interviewed. This allows the producers to see you in action. It will give them a sense of how you perform on camera. For radio producers, include a CD or cassette tape. This allows them to hear your voice and determine how you might perform on air.

For the print media (newspapers and magazines), you may include the video and CD recordings, or you can leave them out. It doesn't really matter unless the recordings are specifically related to your news angle.

10. It may be used to generate multiple stories.

With all of these possibilities before you, it only makes sense to beef up your press kit and make it as captivating and interesting as possible.

The press release in your media kit might be published as is, giving you a little attention somewhere on an inside page. However, if your other documents are intriguing and compelling, the reporter might contact you for a follow-up story, one that may land on the front page. The end result is two stories being published instead of one. This is especially true on slow news days. Again, I speak from experience. On more than one occasion, I've read through a press kit and stumbled upon a hidden gem. I thought, "Wow! Here's the story." I'd push the press release aside and begin working on a story that was much bigger than the one suggested by the press release.

With all of these possibilities before you, it only makes sense to beef up your press kit and make it as captivating and interesting as possible. If you remember to keep it filled with news and well-packaged in a professional manner, you will not be ignored by the press.

Chapter 5

5 Simple Steps to Writing the Ultimate Press Release
How to Turn Your Press Document into a Direct Response Marketing Tool

WHAT IS THE EASIEST WAY, SHORT OF COMMITTING A CRIME, TO get yourself or your business featured in newspapers or magazines?" asks marketing expert Marcia Yudkin. "Just write and send the media a press release."

Do you need to expand your client base but don't have the budget for launching an expensive advertising campaign? Would you like to reach prospects on a local, regional, or national level and promote your products or services at minimum cost?

If you answered yes, then I invite you to consider using a press release. Through a good press release, you can get free mentions in publications that would cost thousands of dollars were you to buy that same space in advertising.

The Ultimate Press Release

Done right, the press release can help start a marketing sensation, which could generate leads from some of the most unsuspecting prospects. However, to make this happen, you need what I call "the ultimate press release," which is not the typical stuff you send to the media. Then what is it?

I define it as a well-written news item about your business that targets a particular audience, reaches the right media, and is published as a news story—and a direct response document.

Some writers and businesspeople are satisfied to simply see print, to get their name in papers and magazines for the purpose of building a clip file. The appearance in prestigious publications is not without merit as it does make for a nice presentation during annual board meetings. The clips will also look good in a portfolio or as part of a proposal or press kit.

I challenge you to think of your press release as a direct response tool. Think of generating prospects, collecting names, and expanding your base.

While the free exposure will certainly enhance your credibility, the publication does not necessarily result in immediate returns of leads or sales. This is why I invite you to try something different. From this day on, I challenge you to think of your press release as a direct response tool. Think of generating prospects, collecting names, and expanding your base. Think ... *ultimate.*

In other words, think about the most efficient way to reach people—in the most cost-effective way—while building a list with the least amount of pressure.

A Direct Response Tool

For the writer or businessperson who wants to see profits ... who wants to see leads and have a powerful presence among prospects and clients, the press release must do more than find print. It has to work as a direct response document; something that will aid you in developing a mailing list.

"Is this really possible?" you ask. Most definitely ... with the right press release.

Here are some thoughts to help you create a press release that generates leads and sells products and services.

1. Determine what publications you'd like to be featured in.

Is it *The Washington Post*? *The New York Times*? *The Saturday Evening Post*? *Newsweek*? Local and regional newspapers?

Once you decide on the media, it would be wise to study those outlets. Understand their style, their focus, their needs. It also would help to contact them and ask for their guidelines and the names of the people who handle what you'd like to offer.

2. Write a statement that opens and closes with news.

As a veteran newsman, I can tell you that legitimate publications do not like fluff or advertisements posing as news. The key is to nail down the news angle of your cause and present it like a news story.

Are you launching a new campaign? Are you running for office? Are you publishing a book? Have you made an unusual impact on a community or country? Are you building a monument? Or expanding your offices? The list could go on.

The key is to nail down the news angle of your cause and present it like a news story.

3. Stress the news in your headline and opening paragraph.

Like the headline in an ad, your headline should grab attention. It should tease the editors and pull them into your copy. As with most forms of writing, it should be clear and succinct.

Do the same with the opening paragraph. In as few words as possible, provide the five Ws and H: Who, what, why, where, when, and how. If possible, tell your story in a single page. If editors want more, they'll request it.

4. Slant your headline for appropriate audiences.

Allow me to use an example from my own work.

In addition to my work in copywriting and journalism, I write religious pamphlets called "gospel tracts." After years of writing them for leading Christian publishers, I decided to launch my own tract ministry.

At first I considered advertising in various Christian magazines and newspapers. But after looking at the cost, I changed my mind and fell back on the press release. Believe me, it was much cheaper, especially on the Internet.

In order to reach three different audiences, I wrote three different headlines:

- For the general audience, found through regular newspapers, I wrote: "Award-winning journalist turns 'Tractster.'"
- Since I served in the Army National Guard, I targeted military magazines with the headline: "Soldier turns 'Tractster.'"
- I had another challenge for the *Church of God Evangel*, a monthly magazine published by the Church of God (Cleveland, TN). I was no longer a member of that denomination; but since I had graduated from one of its schools, East Coast Bible College (Charlotte, NC), I used my school ties as the angle. I wrote: "ECBC graduate authors new tracts."

43

The release was published with both my photograph and the covers of two of my tracts. More importantly, however, it included a direct response element, which brings me to my next point.

5. Make a free offer.

In my press release, I offered free samples of my tracts to anyone who would contact me. Included were my phone number, mailing address, and e-mail address. The piece ran in 2000, and I am still receiving requests for tracts and building up my mailing list at the same time.

I got that idea from Robert W. Bly, the master copywriter and author of more than 50 books, including *Targeted Public Relations* and *Selling Your Services*. "One of the most effective public relations strategies is to send out a press release offering a free booklet, report, or other useful information," he said.

Think of what you can offer. You could highlight it in your headline or opening, making it the focus of your news. Or you may focus on another news item and offer the free product in the body or conclusion of your release. Either way, it's important to offer something that will induce a response.

It is the offer that will make prospects respond. The goal is for them to raise their hands and say they want more information about your service or product.

It is the offer that will make prospects respond. The goal is for them to raise their hands and say they want more information about your service or product. Although news, real news, must be the central focus of the press release, a good offer should be included.

Great offers include FREE information in the form of booklets, product brochures, newsletters, audio or video tapes, etc. Use strong benefit headlines that promise something special for the readers.

Example: "Local manufacturer offers free tips for cleaning pumps." Here's another one, tailored for a national audience: "Pennsylvania car dealer authors new booklet for first-time buyers. Free copies given to first 100 callers." One more: "New guide shows managers how to save money and recruit better workers in a down economy."

As you would expect, all relevant contact information should also be included. Now, will all publications use this information? Probably not. But many will. Either way, it's worth a shot.

When you create a press release that includes the above elements, you'll increase your chances of getting more than publicity. You'll sell products or get valuable leads that just might convert into longtime customers.

Chapter 6

15 Tips for Handling the Press Interview

How to Present Yourself—and Promote Your Cause or Business—in the Best Possible Light

S O WHAT DO YA DO WHEN A REPORTER COMES A CALLIN'?" THE WOMAN asked me. "Lord, I'd be scared out of my wits."

This woman had volunteered to handle publicity for a fire department. Yet, like many people, she was nervous at the thought of speaking to the press.

As a reporter, I'm always amazed at the power (or the perceived power) possessed by the news media. It's always interesting to see how the rich and powerful become shy and timid in the presence of an unassuming writer. Over the years, I've seen many CEOs literally sweat (from being nervous) while answering a few softball questions.

What to Do When a Reporter Calls

Having anxiety about a press interview may be normal, but it doesn't have to ruin your promotional campaign. The suggestions that follow will help you to keep a cool head, answer tough questions, and get the most out of your press interview. Follow this advice and you will know exactly what to do when a reporter "comes a callin'."

Note: Most of the examples you'll see in this section are based on my most recent experiences as a reporter for a daily newspaper in Pennsylvania.

1. Be prepared.

You've heard the old saying, "If you fail to plan, you plan to fail." Well, it's true when it comes to the press interview. Indeed, nothing can take the place of preparation. So before reaching out to the press (in hopes of an interview), make sure of the following:

I challenge you to think of your press release as a direct response tool. Think of generating prospects, collecting names, and expanding your base.

- ▶ Know your topic.
- ▶ Review your notes.
- ▶ Have press documents ready for the reporter.
- ▶ Develop sound bites around your theme or slogan.
- ▶ Rehearse your presentation.
- ▶ Create a list of questions for the media (especially TV and radio).
- ▶ Anticipate questions.

I recently interviewed a woman about an awards banquet. When I arrived at the event, she met me at the door and immediately provided me with a package of information about the event. After the interview, she pointed to the package and said, "This should answer other questions you may have."

That woman was well prepared and she made my day!

2. Be reachable.

I became frustrated when I had to interview a man about an upcoming Christmas event. I had been given his phone number and e-mail address, both of which were connected to the school where he worked.

I called and left a message and I sent e-mails, but he did not respond. Finally, someone told me he'd gone on vacation. So I asked if he had a cell phone, which he did. Two hours before my deadline I made contact.

This guy was hard to reach. Had I failed to make contact, his story would not have made the paper. You can avoid this situation by providing the press with *all* of your contact information. Include: home phone, work phone, cell phone, fax, and e-mail address.

3. Be flexible.

Today, many reporters use e-mail for their interviews. Surprisingly, however, some people insist on face-to-face interviews. Consider this example:

I'd sent a list of questions to a woman about an upcoming musical. For two days I checked my e-mail box in search of her answers. Then, 30 minutes before my deadline, she called me.

"Did you receive the questions I sent by e-mail?" I asked.

"Yes, but I thought you were coming to see me. I don't like writing. I prefer working face-to-face."

Well, I took her information over the phone and wrote the story as quickly as possible. The published piece was OK, but it would have been better if I had more time. Much more could have been done with the story had the subject been more flexible—more accommodating. Even more, she could have enjoyed better publicity for her event.

The key is to nail down the news angle of your cause and present it like a news story.

4. Be efficient.

I was interviewing a woman about a support group for military families who had loved ones serving in Iraq. She presented me with a newsletter with valuable information for my story.

"May I have a copy of this?" I asked.

She paused. "Ah … this is my only copy."

She immediately turned to a friend and said, "I have a copier at home. Give me 15 minutes and I'll run home and make you a copy."

The woman proved to be very efficient, a quality that means a lot to a busy reporter.

On another assignment, I was interviewing a woman about a holiday event when I asked questions that she could not answer. So she quickly gave me the name and contact information of the person who could help me. She later called me back to see if I had other questions and whether I'd succeeded in reaching the other person.

Make no mistake. Efficiency goes a long way. It helps reporters to do better and allows you to get the publicity you need for your business.

5. Be honest.

There is a Scripture that states, "Be sure your sins will find you out." That's especially true when talking to reporters.

For this reason, it behooves you to be honest and truthful in every way. There's no need to pretend or to exaggerate. If you do, it will certainly come to light.

If you don't know something or you're unsure, simply say so. The reporter will appreciate your honesty. This will also save you from any embarrassing moments down the road.

6. Be yourself.

This advice may be simple, but it is relevant, nonetheless. In short, avoid "acting" and pretending to be what you are not. Good reporters can read you and see through the facade.

In a worst-case scenario, a reporter will note your fake pretense and mention it in a story. Imagine the embarrassment.

7. Be patient.

It is the offer that will make prospects respond. The goal is for them to raise their hands and say they want more information about your service or product.

Although some reporters use tape recorders, most use only their pen and notebook. For this reason, it helps to speak slowly and clearly when making comments. Give the reporter time to take down notes. Sometimes reporters will ask you to repeat yourself so they can make sure they understand what you're saying. If this happens in your case, don't fret. It's good, because the reporter wants to get it right. At other times, they may ask you to spell a name. When this happens, be prepared to use letter association, such as "a" as in "apple" or "b" as in "bravo." And so on.

8. Be clear.

Sometimes a reporter will ask a question that will leave you stumped. Or he or she will use terms that you are not familiar with. When this happens, simply ask the reporter to repeat the question. Or you could say, "I'm not sure I follow you."

If the reporter speaks about anything you don't understand, feel free to say you don't understand.

9. Be firm.

From time to time a reporter will ask you a few hard questions. If you cannot address the questions, just say so and stick to your guns. Another approach would be to say, "I'd love to comment on this, but it would not be appropriate at this time." Or, you could say you're not really comfortable or authorized to speak about the issue.

Smart reporters will hardly take no for an answer. They will persist and try to ask the question in more ways than one. So be prepared and be firm. No means no.

10. Be colorful.

Like most people, reporters love a good story. So when answering questions, try to include a couple of interesting stories or anecdotes to support your point of view. Cite one of the books of quotations, mention a poem, reference a popular movie. Or simply share a personal story. It can be funny or serious. Just make sure that it helps to shed light on your comments.

11. Be thorough.

If you can help it, avoid "yes" and "no" answers. Try to explain yourself in detail. Reach for good illustrations or analogies. Do whatever you can for the sake of clarity.

Don't worry about talking too much or sharing too much. Reporters love information and they would rather have too much, than too little. After all, they are masters of eating the meat and spitting out the bones.

12. Be professional.

Being professional is crucial for earning respect and winning over a reporter. So avoid the things that can really tick them off. To help, I've included a few "don'ts."

Don't ask to read the story before it goes to press. For starters, this is the question of an amateur. People who have worked with the media know it is against company policy for reporters to use the featured subject as an editor. Some reporters find it insulting. Why? It suggests they can't be trusted to do a good job.

Don't insult reporters by telling them how to do their job. I was interviewing a successful businessman once when he tried to tell me how to "frame" my story. I'll never forget it. Here's how it started:

"Now when you mention this, be sure to write it this way ..." he said. "Tell it like this."

When my photographer began to snap pictures, the businessman stood up. "I was pretty good with a camera once," he said. "Don't take any of me sitting over there. Let's go to this other office. I want people to see me with this painting in the background."

And on he went.

Suffice it to say, that while he may have been a good businessman, he did not make friends and influence people on that day.

Don't engage in name-calling. Just recently I interviewed a Civil War re-enactor who was dressed as a Confederate soldier. When I was about to leave, he said, "You ain't part of the liberal media, are ya?"

I looked at him. "Excuse me?" I said. "Where did that come from?"

He tried to explain himself but it was too late. The damage was done. I was tempted to drop the story altogether, but I was on a deadline and had no other source I could call.

Don't criticize the messenger or the media. When I arrived at a banquet to do a story about local volunteer firefighters, one of the volunteers said, "Come on in. So you work for the local fish-wrapper, huh?"

He thought he was being funny. Surprisingly, one of his colleagues heard him and began to criticize every fire and rescue story the paper had published within the last week.

Of course, I had a job to do. So I ignored them. But I'll never forget them. And neither will the reporters who interview you.

Don't go off track. Stay on the topic at hand. You may have interesting bits to share about yourself or people you know, but keep the focus on the reporter's questions.

As I write this I'm reminded of an interview I conducted with an administrator of a local hospital. As we talked, I learned that he had some fascinating personal experiences. But since I was there to help him promote the hospital—and not his own achievements—he abruptly ended all talk about himself.

"OK," he said. "Enough about me. Let's talk about the real story."

That's a good example to follow.

13. Be personable.

When the reporter arrives for the interview, make him or her feel right at home. And don't underestimate the power of a compliment. If you like the reporter's coat, tie, hair, finger nails, etc., feel free to offer a compliment. If you enjoyed one of the reporter's stories in the past, mention this and let the reporter know how much you liked it.

Am I suggesting you kiss up to the reporter? Of course. Just be sincere.

Also, avoid being stiff and formal as if you're on trial. Be friendly and warm. Ask questions of the reporter and talk about other things to warm the atmosphere. This will put both of you at ease.

I'll never forget the time I went to the home of a pianist. I had a bad cold and was struggling to suppress my coughing. Well, the elderly lady I was assigned to interview, noticed I was sick. So before the interview, she made a cup of tea. "Try this," she said. "It should make you feel better."

As I sipped the tea, she asked about my family and how I liked living in the area. When I was done, she played the piano. The interview followed.

After the story appeared, she sent me a kind "thank you" note with best wishes for my health.

14. Be generous.

Remember this cardinal rule: If you do what you can to make the reporter's job easy, you'll stand a greater chance of getting the publicity you need.

That said, be willing to give tips for news that's unrelated to your story. Give the reporter names and contact information.

When you show you are knowledgeable about an issue, the reporter will remember you in the future. You may even be invited to write a column.

15. Be reliable.

Strive to be a source that reporters can trust—a source that they call on anytime they need a quote.

Some years ago, I became acquainted with a guy who worked for the Edward Jones Company. He became valuable to our paper because he was a constant source of news related to his industry. If he read a story that was not clear about investments, he would call me or send an e-mail to share how the issue could be better explained.

If he heard of something that might have been of interest to the paper, he would give me a call. Sometimes he would send me a page from a national publication and say, "I thought you'd be interested in this."

Well, after doing this for about a year, my paper began using him as a news analyst. Whenever we reported on something involving his line of work, we'd call him for his opinion. In short, this businessman proved himself and stood out from his competitors because he was not only knowledgeable, but reliable. We could count on him anytime we needed an expert's opinion.

Build on the Experience

After you've had an interview with a reporter, you have the opportunity to cultivate that relationship. You can begin by asking the reporter to contact you if he or she has any questions or needs more information.

Once the story is published, send a "thank you" card or letter. This means a great deal to reporters.

Throughout the year, as you read other work by the reporter, send notes to offer compliments about various stories. If you learn of something hot, or something that could become a major story, kindly provide the reporter with the tip.

When these suggestions become a normal part of your promotional campaign, you will be overwhelmed with the media coverage and publicity you'll receive.

Chapter 7

9 Easy Ways to Beef Up Your Web Site for Maximum Exposure

Proven and Effective Ways to Get the Most from Internet Technology

A YOUNG BUSINESSMAN HAD CREATED A WEB SITE FOR HIS COMPUTER technology service and he could hardly hold back the excitement as he showed me his homepage.

"Can you believe it? Look at this!" he said, grinning.

I watched as a series of stars appeared. The background gradually changed from black, to red and to a number of other colors. Then there was music, something from a "Star Wars" movie. Eventually, pictures faded in and out.

I was still waiting.

"Check it out, check it out," my friend said.

Slowly, a few words appeared on the screen … then faded out and morphed into colorful designs. By this time I was concerned. "Is it working?" I asked. "Something wrong?"

"No, no, no," he said. "Just pure technology. Advanced technology. Isn't it cool?"

After what seemed to be two minutes, his homepage—and text—finally emerged.

Charlie Cook, a recognized authority on Internet marketing, says your web site is like a flight of stairs into your business. "Once you've got prospects to your homepage—your online front door—you want to move them to action," he says. "If you miss a step or two, prospects will fall and won't make it in the door to your business."

My friend thought his slow-loading web site was a great marketing tool, but what he had was a common mistake that's made by people who are caught up with graphics, and all the bells and whistles of modern technology. What he didn't realize was that he would enjoy this site far more than his prospects and customers. Indeed, he'd missed some important steps in serving his audience. Being tech savvy is one thing, but knowing how to use it to effectively promote a business is quite another. This section will serve as a checklist for improving your web site. Its aim is to show you how to build it up for maximum traffic, sales, and exposure.

1. Determine your objective.

In determining your objective, it is also important that your web site reflect the image and culture of your company— and the ones you want to project.

As with any other aspect of your campaign, developing—and improving— your web site should begin with an understanding of your purpose. Will it be used to sell products and services? Or will you use it as a resource guide for educational purposes? Do you want it to be a source of news and commentary? Or a tool to promote a single part of your business?

Some web sites desire heavy traffic. But some are set up as merely a portfolio for prospective clients.

In determining your objective, it is also important that your web site reflect the image and culture of your company—and the ones you want to project. In other words, it should not have the feel of an entertainment site or the amateurish gimmicks of a teenager on myspace.com.

With this in mind, begin by asking yourself: What do I want to accomplish? Whom do I want to reach? What impression do I want to make?

2. Do your homework.

Before launching your site, it would help to do your homework. Invest some time in studying your competitors. Make note of their strong points and weak points. See what you like and don't like about their design. Make an analysis to determine what works and what doesn't work for you. What would you change? How can you adapt their strong points to your own design?

But don't stop there. You can also solicit feedback from your customers. Ask them to visit your site and give you their opinion. This will make them feel a part of your enterprise. Of course, it would certainly help to consult with someone who specializes in web site designs.

3. Highlight your slogan—your unique sales message.

Use the "first-thing test" to announce your presence. This means you glance at your web page and ask yourself, "What's the first thing I see when I look at this page?" Chances are, what you see first is what your visitors will see when they review your site. Since your interest is business, the first thing they see should be your sales message.

Since your interest is business, the first thing customers should see at your site should be your sales message.

Place your name (or company name) and slogan at the top of your homepage. This will allow visitors to know in an instant who you are and what you do. This will also let them know if they're at the right place.

If you have a particular product you want to highlight, you can place this at the top of the page. For instance, author Jay Abraham used to feature a thumbnail of one of his books. Visitors could click on it for more details. When Joe Vitale's book defeated *Harry Potter* for the number one spot on Amazon.com, Joe adjusted his homepage by turning it into a press release. This was major news and it served him well.

On the other hand, Bob Bly uses his name and title at the top of his web site, just above a colorful burst that invites visitors to use his copywriting services. When you visit his site, the first things you see are his name (which is well-known) and his call to action.

However, until you are as well-known as Bly, I'd encourage you to highlight your most important sales message, followed by an explanation of how you or your business can help prospects achieve their goals.

4. Use a newsletter to collect the names of visitors.

If you want to follow up on leads and keep visitors returning, you need a way to collect their e-mail addresses. One of the most effective ways to do this is by offering a free e-zine. For the best results, consider placing the signup box at the top of the page, preferably on the right-hand side. But instead of just saying, "Sign up for our free newsletter," mention a benefit the reader receives by subscribing. Example: "Sign up for FREE newsletter that keeps you up-to-date on _____." Or, "Sign up for FREE newsletter that shows you how to _____." Another option is to offer a free bonus, such as a special report or e-book to all first-time subscribers.

When I signed up for Bob Bly's e-zine, I received a free e-book on copywriting. When I became a subscriber of AbsoluteWrite.com's e-zine, the publisher sent me a free directory of literary agents. Both of these gifts were useful and highly appealing. They demonstrate the effective way of using gifts to pick up subscribers.

5. Be careful with the bells and whistles.

"I enjoy looking at graphics, but not if it takes over 30 boring seconds of staring at a blank screen before the web site comes up," says web expert Hans Klein. "If your web site takes too long to load, [customers] will just click away to another site."

Many web sites are too graphic-rich. They're fun to play with and may be good for pure entertainment. But when it comes to marketing and promotions, this can be too much of an otherwise good thing. Loading time is especially important because many people still have a slow Internet connection. Besides this, they are busy and won't take the time to sit and wait for your pages to appear. Instead, they will move on to another site, perhaps your competitor.

In her book, *Doing Business on the Internet: Big Ideas for Growing Businesses*, Kendra Bennett says less is often more when it comes to promoting your business. "Because the capabilities of the medium are great, it's easy to become a victim of the Web's potential," she writes. "A useful rule of thumb is: Just because you can do something, doesn't automatically mean you have to."

Bennett admonishes businesses to "curb the desire to over-design," and, if necessary, enlist the design advice and expertise of a seasoned professional.

Aim to make your site user-friendly in every sense of the word. Use large type and features that provide easy navigation.

Aim to make your site user-friendly in every sense of the word. Use large type (about 10 to 12 points) and features that provide easy navigation. Try to limit your type to one or two fonts, or maybe three. Ideally, your web pages must guide the customer toward the specific solutions they are looking for. Think of your pages as a map that's easy to follow, with links that guide customers step by step to their destination.

6. Use the motivating sales sequence.

For years marketers have followed the AIDA principle in designing their sales presentations. It stands for: Attention, Interest, Desire, Action. Using this principle, the text must first grab the customer's *attention*, and then create an *interest* in the product or service. It should then turn the interest into a strong *desire* to purchase the product or service. The customer must then be encouraged to take *action* that will lead to a sale.

Your text will be easier to read if it's presented in short sentences and short paragraphs. Use bullets and subheads on each page. Use a friendly, conversational tone. Watch out for jargon and any words not easily understood by your audience.

7. Inject your site with credibility.

People like doing business with people they can trust. Therefore, the more credible you are, the more business you can expect. Besides having a quality product and delivering quality service, your credibility will be enhanced by a list of compelling testimonials.

Use them on your homepage and sprinkle them throughout your other pages. You may also have a separate page entitled, "Testimonials" or "Satisfied Clients." Under this heading, you could write, "What they say about the Anyname Company and its work …"

Another way to strengthen your credibility is to deliver a strong guarantee. Whether it's for 30 days, 90 days, or a year, it should be stated (and highlighted) with as much detail and conviction as possible. If necessary, explain the security features of your site so visitors will feel safe in doing business with you.

8. Make it easy for prospects to reach you.

One of the most frustrating things I encounter with some web sites is the time it takes to locate a phone number and mailing address. I recently had problems with two well-known companies and needed to talk to a live person. Before I could find their phone numbers, I had to go through a series of links in the "Help" section. In all, I spent about 30 minutes answering questions and moving through pages. Eventually, the phone number was given. I became so frustrated that when I called the number, I cancelled the service.

If possible, include your full contact information at the bottom of each page, as well as in the "Contact" section.

Don't you make this same mistake. Instead, make it easy for visitors to reach you. If possible, include your full contact information at the bottom of each page, as well as in the "Contact" section. Doing this will not only allow you to answer your visitors' questions, but it will also enhance your credibility.

About a year ago, when I was searching for a reliable Internet Service Provider, my first question was, "Can I reach you by phone if I have a problem?" I selected the one that guaranteed their accessibility.

9. Make it a one-stop shop for essential resources related to your business.

Look around and you'll find that the most successful web sites have much to offer. In addition to basic information about company services and products, these web sites include tons of free articles, newsletters, blogs, news, e-books, and a number of sources not mentioned here. Your web site can benefit from this same approach.

In addition to basic information about company services and products, successful web sites include tons of free articles, newsletters, blogs, news, e-books, and a number of sources not mentioned here.

Take the lead in your field. Be the expert in your market. Give visitors the things they need and want. Besides the items listed above, inject your resource page with case studies and commentary on current events. Explain how the news relates to your audience. Report on the latest research relating to your products and services. This can be done through articles or in a blog.

And don't forget product reviews and a list of recommended resources. To show objectivity, be generous in citing your sources and in providing links to their web pages. Doing this will practically guarantee your status as a leader in your field. Before long, even the media will begin using your resources and quoting you in print and over the airways.

See Marked Improvements

Now, having read these tips, you may wonder if they're your ticket to quick riches. No, implementing these ideas may not make you the next Internet giant, certainly not the next Bill Gates. But what you can expect is a marked improvement in your sales, traffic, and exposure before your audience. Will this occur overnight? Hardly. As with any venture, it usually takes time. But as you experiment with different features and measure your results, your time will not be wasted.

Chapter 8

8 Important Facts About Publishing Newsletters
Tapping a Low-Cost Medium to Reach Your Audience on a Regular Basis

I HAVE ALWAYS BEEN A FAN OF NEWSLETTERS, BUT SOMETHING OCCURRED IN my business that made me appreciate them even more as a tool for promotional campaign.

In the winter of 1999, I made a bold statement about my plans to become well-known as a copywriter in the fundraising industry. At the time, I wanted to step away from the daily grind of journalism and spend more time as an independent copywriter. But to succeed, I needed clients. So I devised a plan that would get my name out before the masses. Here's what I told a friend:

"Right now, I'm an unknown in this field. But I promise you, within one year from today, I'll be well-known by all the key names in the business. And I'll have some of them as clients."

My friend smiled and asked how I would pull it off. So I explained.

I would self-publish a four-page newsletter called *Expert Marketing* that would position me as an expert in my field. It would have a professionally designed banner and include my photo; the rest of it would be typewritten and have three holes punched in the left-hand margin. Each issue would consist of a single how-to article and a brief bio about my services and contact information. I explained how I would send the newsletter out to 100 of the top people in my field and to 50 magazine editors and newsletter publishers.

Well, I implemented this plan and within two days, I received a fax from George Reis, editor of *Fund Raising Management* magazine, inviting me to write a monthly column. The next day, I heard from a business in Texas asking me to write a direct mail package for the company. An author called and requested permission to excerpt the newsletter in an upcoming book. The week following, two editors of small business publications invited me to write columns for their monthly magazines.

To make a long story short, my plan worked, although sooner than expected. Instead of becoming well-known within a year, I made a name for myself within weeks.

The publication of my column in *Fund Raising Management* had other benefits as well. In addition to enhancing my image as an authority, it boosted my client list and allowed me to sell other writing products. Beyond that, it allowed me to charge more for my copywriting services. I'll never forget the reaction of Richard Armstrong when I told him about the news.

"Wow, you're famous!" he said. "Now you have the credibility of an expert. So charge like an expert." He suggested some figures and explained that if I charged less, people would not take me seriously. I took his advice and have been happy ever since.

The experience I had with this form of communication has given me some insight and a few lessons that I want to share with you.

1. Position your business in the marketplace.

Establishing your name as a leader in your field may be one of the most important reasons for launching a newsletter.

Establishing your name as a leader in your field may be one of the most important reasons for launching a newsletter. If this is your aim, then use the newsletter to portray your name and business in the best light. Begin with a clever name and tag line. Use a name that expresses your unique sales message and one that differentiates you from the competition. Include your photograph in each issue. Highlight testimonials and endorsements.

Do your research and write like an expert. Give insight that is found nowhere else. Become the one-stop shop for what your audience needs and wants in your field. Be the person your clients and customers will recommend to others. Be alert and keep them abreast of breaking news that relates to your products or service. Show them how current events or the "evening news" can affect their lives. In other words, become the "guru" whom they will look to for answers and advice.

Whenever you earn a new credential or special award, mention it in the publication and explain what it means in terms of better service for your audience. By doing this on a regular basis, your status as an expert will be cemented in their thinking.

2. Build customer loyalty.

Since the newsletter allows you to have constant contact with your audience, it is an effective tool for nurturing relationships. So use it to find out what your audience likes or dislikes about your products or services. Use it to run surveys. Ask for their recommendations.

Feel free to be personable. Talk about your experiences, as well as theirs. You also may want to report news about some of your readers. Put their names in your publication, and you can count on their loyalty for the long haul.

Since the newsletter allows you to have constant contact with your audience, it is an effective tool for nurturing relationships.

3. Provide solid news and valuable information.

Some marketers make the mistake of having too much promotional copy. They include so many offers that the newsletter is seen as one long sales letter. Don't make this mistake.

Offer your readers solid information that they cannot find anywhere else. Give them tips that will make their lives better. Help them to save money, prevent loss, solve problems, and sell more of their products or services. In short, help them to meet their needs and you will have them for a long time.

In addition to giving how-to information in each issue, add some variety by including case studies, research findings, and inspirational quotes. You could also include book reviews and a list of recommended resources.

4. Promote your products and services.

The newsletter is not only a medium for offering news and how-to information; it is a good resource through which you can sell books, tapes, CDs, special reports, white papers, seminars and workshops.

Practically any product or service you have to offer can be promoted through your newsletter. If you have an upcoming speaking engagement, then use your publication to alert your readers. In fact, you can publish your whole itinerary. You can sweeten the deal by offering special discounts to your subscribers. The same holds true for your books or other products.

5. Offer a premium incentive.

In your direct mail and advertisements, you can offer your newsletter as a FREE bonus to the readers who respond to your "call to action." Example: "If you call today, you will receive a FREE one-year subscription to *The Writing Hustler*, which is valued at $60 a year. This unique resource will help you to improve your copy and sell more of your products and services! Call NOW!"

In your P.S. you could write: "Even if you decide to return the (product), the newsletter is yours to keep."

6. Increase circulation.

In my own case, I wasn't interested in a large subscription base or circulation. I only wanted to reach a select number of people in the fundraising industry. Since the number I wanted to impress was under 100, my newsletter accomplished its goal.

If you want to boost your circulation, there are a number of methods you can use:

- ▶ Run small classifieds in select publications and e-zines.
- ▶ Include it as a free offer in the bio section of your articles.
- ▶ Offer it as a freebie at your speaking engagements.
- ▶ Encourage current subscribers to share the newsletters with their friends and colleagues.

A large circulation provides you with a mailing list that you can tap anytime you want.

A large circulation has many benefits, some of which are obvious. For one thing, it provides you with a mailing list that you can tap anytime you want. Another benefit is that you will become attractive to book publishers who recognize your platform for selling books. If you desire, you could begin charging a fee for the newsletter. At some point, if you wish to sell the newsletter, a large circulation will increase its value.

7. Repackage as a book.

After years of publishing the newsletter, *Publishing Poynters*, self-publishing guru Dan Poynter compiled his newsletter into a book and presented the volume to his readers. This is a common practice among a few newsletter publishers. I encourage you to do the same. Remember: If people will buy your information one way, they will buy it in another format.

The beauty of this approach is that the newsletter may be published for free, but as a book it can be sold.

8. Sell advertisements.

When your newsletter reaches a high circulation figure, it will be attractive to advertisers who want to reach your audience. While this certainly is not mandatory, it is a legitimate way to generate extra income.

Since a newsletter is part of your promotional campaign, it would help to include the media in your distribution. After you have established a name for yourself, don't be surprised when you see the media quoting from your publication. This could lead to interviews and television appearances, as well as untapped prospects and loyal customers.

Chapter 9

10 Quick Tips for Designing a Promotional Brochure

How to Use the Essential Elements of Advertising to Create an Attractive and Persuasive Document

I N A PRESENTATION ABOUT THE USE OF MEDIA KITS AS PROMOTIONAL TOOLS, a well-known speaker gave a list of items that should be used in the kit. Surprisingly, her list did not include brochures.

Why? "Presentation folders have replaced them," she said.

Well, I strongly disagree. And for many reasons.

The truth of the matter is, brochures are more popular than this speaker realizes. In fact, many businesses—large and small—consistently use brochures because of their effectiveness, and their convenience. For most, simply having a brochure suggests credibility, according to copywriter Bob Bly, because having one is expected—and it shows you're in business. As a promotional tool, a brochure can be practically any size and shape. It can be plain or full of color, all text or filled with graphics.

It can be used as a "leave behind" after meeting with a prospect or as an insert in a direct mail package. It can stand alone or work to support your advertising and other documents in your campaign. It can answer questions, clarify issues, and offer solutions. Because of its flexibility in size, it can be

64

quite handy for people on the go. It will fit in a pocket or purse, and may be handed out in airports, cabs, tradeshows, or on the streets like religious tracts. And yes, it may also be included with your media kit.

Since a brochure is essentially an informational tool, it can be used to describe your products and services in detail, while explaining how they work. It may also include background information on you or your company.

Do you currently use brochures to market your products or services? Would you like to give your brochures a makeover for maximum results? If so, then read on and discover what you can do to make your brochure a winner.

1. Use a compelling headline on the front cover.

In the same way you would write a headline for an ad or a title for a book, write a clever, provocative headline for the cover of your brochure. The headline could be a question or teaser, or it could promise a benefit. It may also include your unique sales message, or address a need or problem that your audience wants to solve.

"The success of an entire advertising campaign may stand or fall on what is said in the headlines of the individual advertisements," wrote John Caples in his classic, *Tested Advertising Methods*. He cited an article in which writer Don Belding wrote, "Inquiry returns show that the headline is 50 to 75 percent of the advertisement. So selling punch in your headline is about the most important thing."

In the same way you would write a headline for an ad or a title for a book, write a clever, provocative headline for the cover of your brochure.

The best headlines are those that appeal to the reader's self-interest. They offer news, pique curiosity, and suggest easy, quick ways to accomplish something. With this in mind, use a headline that will move the reader to turn the page and begin reading. Personally, I like using "How to" whenever I can, because it works—and the promise of a benefit is clear. Of course, I try to tie this to the unique sales message of my business.

2. Organize your selling points.

If your purpose is to lead the reader to a sale, or to contact you for more information, use the AIDA principle to guide him or her along the way. AIDA stands for Attention, Interest, Desire, and Action. First you grab attention and then you create interest in your product or service. Next, you inspire a desire and then encourage the reader to take action.

The information you provide should flow seamlessly from one point to the next and from one page to the next, all leading to the call to action. The structure you use will be determined by your objectives and the type of product or service you're promoting. In general, however, you might use an outline such as this:

- ▶ Introduction
- ▶ Benefits
- ▶ Product or service offered
- ▶ Features
- ▶ Application
- ▶ Testimonials
- ▶ Question and Answer
- ▶ Fees and Terms of Condition
- ▶ Biographical or History
- ▶ Call to action
- ▶ Coupon (optional)

How much of this you include will also depend on the size and format of your publication. In most instances, a "slim jim" (8½ x 11 sheet, folded in thirds) will work just fine. For larger publications, 11x17, folded with four panels might be preferred. Of course, some brochures are much larger and have the appearance of a small catalog. The smaller versions, however, are less expensive and more suitable for carrying. They also make a nice fit for direct mail packages using business-sized envelopes.

When you begin writing the copy for your brochure, be sure to answer the who, what, why, how, where, and when.

3. Break up topics into short sections.

When you begin writing the copy for your brochure, be sure to answer the who, what, why, how, where, and when—the same information you would include in a press release. Organize your copy so that it can be read quickly. Aim for clarity.

In most cases, when people pick up your brochure, they will likely read it the way they would a book: They'll look at the front cover, turn it over and review the back cover, and then open it to review the inside.

Your inside copy will be more engaging if you break up topics into short sections. Use headlines and subheads on each page. Underline words and sentences (or use all caps) for emphasis. Use color, arrows, and boxes to direct the reader to key points. Bullets and numbers for your points make them easy to see, easy to read, and easy to scan. Use them where appropriate.

4. Use a photo that supports your message.

In advertising, copy is king. So what you write should have priority—and be prominent—in your brochure. Graphics in the form of photographs, drawings, charts, and other images are vital, but they should support and enhance the writing, and not the other way around. Use images that direct the reader's eye to key headlines or benefits. For products, use images that illustrate how the product is used.

For your cover, a single picture is preferred. In fact, research shows that one large photo on the cover is more effective than multiple images. Also, according to advertising specialists Kenneth Roman and Jane Mass, an illustration that has story appeal and bright colors will involve the reader.

Use images that direct the reader's eye to key headlines or benefits.

5. Pour on the facts.

Jay Conrad Levinson, noted author of *Guerrilla Marketing*, says the format of a brochure is not nearly as important as the content. "The content must be factual information, enlivened with a touch of style and romance," he says. "Unlike ads, which must flag a person's attention, a brochure or circular already has that attention. So its primary job is to inform with the intention of selling."

Use your brochure to provide every detail that will move the reader to action. This is especially vital if your brochure is used as a direct response tool, or as part of a direct mail package. Attempt to answer questions and any objections the reader may have.

If you're featuring a complex product, explain in detail how it works. Use illustrated drawings and photographs to make your information clear. If you're providing a service, show the reader how the service operates and the benefits it offers. Discuss payment plans and terms or conditions. Talk about your guarantee and your return policy.

6. Make it credible.

There are a number of proven ways to infuse your brochure with credibility and authenticity. Sometimes the quality of paper, expert design and layout, and the quality of writing will enhance your credibility. Below are four other ways to get the credibility you want:

▶ First, begin with specifics and avoid generalities. Instead of describing your product in general terms and estimates, use concrete language that tells exactly what your product does and the specific benefits the reader will receive.

▶ Second, use research and statistics. Is your product (or its benefits) supported by current research? Do you have surveys or polls to back up your claim? If so, then give this information a prominent place in your brochure.

▶ Third, use testimonials by experts and satisfied customers/clients. Pepper your pages with highlighted quotes or use a single panel with a full list of quotes.

▶ Fourth, use a strong guarantee, a compelling one that will not be questioned. Assure the reader that if he or she is not satisfied, he or she can return the product or receive free technical assistance for six months, or be given the option to try another product at no cost, etc. In other words, place yourself in the shoes of the consumer and think of what you would want if you were not satisfied with a product or service. How would you want to be treated?

7. Make it client/customer-centered.

Because you are proud of your achievements and you want the world to know how good your business is, it is easy to get carried away and write everything about *you*. But keep in mind, your prospects and customers are only concerned about themselves and what you can do for them. So it goes without saying that your brochure, while describing who you are and what you offer, should focus primarily on what matters to your audience. In short, your writing should be client/customer-centered.

While describing who you are and what you offer, should focus primarily on what matters to your audience.

"More than 90 percent of the marketing documents I review are about the seller rather than the buyer ...." writes Dr. Jeffrey Lant in *Cash Copy*. "What matters in marketing is relentlessly focusing on your prospect—in each and every way. Your own professional image should always be secondary to your ability to convince your prospect that you place his welfare first; that you can deliver benefit after benefit he'll find meaningful and that persuade him to buy what you're selling."

8. Make it worth keeping.

When people receive your brochure, whether by mail or through personal face-to-face distribution, they will do one of four things: (1) they might read it and take action; (2) they might save it for later; (3) they might give it to someone else; or (4) they might throw it away.

You want your readers to avoid throwing it away. And you can prevent this and extend the life of your brochure by making it a valuable document that's worth saving. How is this done? There are a number of ways:

▶ Include a list of tips or practical how-to information that address a need or desire of your audience. For instance, you could offer "15 ways to save money on your next home"; "10 ways to rid your garden of rodents"; "7 things you should know about finding a new job"; "10 important ways to keep a good employee"; "8 tips for getting the most out of your mutual fund."

▶ Include a list of valuable resources with contact information. When a nonprofit group wanted to pressure Congress about an issue that concerned their town, they sent out a mailing that included a brochure with all of the names and contact information of their representatives. Some of the recipients I know threw the letter away, but they kept the brochure and even shared it with others. One person said, "Another issue will come up soon and I can use this list to reach the right people."

▶ As an authority on a certain subject, you can include a list of important resources to help your readers achieve their goals. This could be a list of vendors, web sites, e-zines, or even a list of other experts, along with their contact information. If you sell a certain computer product, you could list all of the software and tools that are compatible to the product.

▶ Have the design play an important role. For example, you can turn your brochure into a calendar with pictures and your sales message presented on each page. Or you can use a brochure that doubles as a poster that's suitable for framing.

9. Don't forget the obvious.

The most obvious feature of any brochure is the contact information. Unfortunately, in a fast-paced working environment, it's easy to forget things we take for granted. So once you have completed your final draft, proofread and check to ensure your full (and correct) contact information is included.

I know of one company that included the wrong phone number in its brochure, which was used in a direct mail package. A few days after the mailing, calls began pouring in to an office number that had nothing to do with the products being promoted. The customer service department waited anxiously to receive calls. Unfortunately, their expected calls were going to another number.

Some marketers include the web address in tiny print at the bottom of each page, which is not a bad idea. If your brochure includes a coupon, print the address on both the coupon and on another page inside the brochure. This way, when the coupon is removed, the reader will still know how to reach you.

Once you have completed your final draft, proofread and check to ensure your full (and correct) contact information is included.

10. Tell the reader what to do.

Whatever it is you want prospects to do must be spelled out in clear and precise terms.

Think about what you want the reader to do. Do you want him or her to write or call you for more information? Do you want them to stop by your store for a special discount? Whatever it is you want prospects to do must be spelled out in clear and precise terms.

"Every brochure should have a clear call to action," say the authors of *How to Advertise*. Without this important feature, you have a wasted opportunity.

Experience of a Tax Collector

When I think about the uses of a brochure as a marketing tool, I'm reminded of a friend who was elected as a tax collector in a Pennsylvania town. Unlike his opponent, my friend used a brochure to help get his message across. He created a simple black-and-white, four-page brochure. At the top of the front cover, he used the headline, "Why You Should Vote for _____ as Tax Collector." His photo appeared just underneath the headline. Inside he gave four good reasons that resonated with the people in his area. My friend campaigned door-to-door, distributing his brochure to each home. On Election Day, he unseated a longtime incumbent and became the town's new tax collector.

After the election, I asked a number of people about the results and why they believed he won. More than one said, "He had a good brochure."

Chapter 10

10 Pointers for Using Tip Sheets and Articles for Lasting Exposure

How to Enhance Your Credibility as an Expert in Your Field

YOU MAY HAVE WRITTEN AND SENT OUT HUNDREDS OF PRESS RELEASES over the years. But what about tip sheets? Or general articles? When was the last time you had one published?

For the next few minutes, I want to drive home the importance of using tip sheets and articles as a vital tool in your promotional campaign. Though sometimes neglected by some business professionals, it is a powerful way for you to increase your visibility, while enhancing your credibility.

Tip sheets are those brief, quick-and-dirty articles that use bullets or numbers to provide useful information in an easy-to-read form. Whether you read consumer, trade, or religious publications, you see tip sheets or list articles dominating the pages. The reason for their prominence in so many publications is that they work. Some marketers know this and practice it all the time. However, all too often, this tool is left aside as something only "real" writers can do.

Now this can change. And it should, because practically any business can deliver practical, useful articles on a regular basis. "Writing an article automatically puts you at the top of the experts' list," noted publicity expert Raleigh Pinskey. "It's very good visibility, reaching thousands of prospects in one effort."

Unlike the press release, published articles have more credibility. People clip them out and save them. They pass them on to other readers. In many cases, the articles generate income for the writers.

As a journalist, I can tell you that newspapers crave tip sheets and how-to articles, especially when they're putting out a special supplement. Another reason for their interest in the form is that journalists love to quote experts—a title reserved for a few respected writers and industry leaders.

With this in mind, I think it's easy to see why some people are called on by the national media to speak with a voice of authority. Publishing tip sheets and how-to articles gives you such a platform.

As I was preparing this section, I looked around for a good book, a solid guide that would help any business professional—on any level—to get tip sheets and articles published. Luckily, I came across a short book that's packed with user-friendly advice. It's called, *A Writer's Guide to Magazine Articles for Book Promotion and Profit* by Patricia L. Fry.

Fry has been a professional writer for more than 27 years. During this time, she has coached and taught many writers how to improve their work and how to get published. She's been on the front lines of the writing business for a number of organizations. And she's authored a number of books.

Her book gives you all the nuts and bolts to getting published. In addition to explaining the need for publishing articles, it provides you with tips for recognizing good ideas. It also shows you, step by step, how to take an idea, develop it, and then place it with a publication. Good strategies also are given for dealing with editors. A good list of writing and publishing resources—online and offline—is included.

1. Articles can be used for nonprofits and any other organization.

In an interview with Fry, I asked her about using articles to promote a nonprofit group. And she agreed it should be done.

"I certainly use a lot of non-profit organizations as resources when I write articles on various topics," she said. "I used several in my piece for *The World and I* on how America is helping our kids."

Fry also interviewed directors of nonprofit groups for articles featuring therapeutic gardening, how to care for the caregiver, neighborhood mentors for children, grandparenting, feral cats, and many, many others.

As far as specific groups who have attempted to gain higher visibility through articles, Fry has done that herself. In fact, she has successfully written articles to promote SPAWN (Small Publishers, Artists, and Writers Network).

"I was in on the ground floor of this non-profit organization," she said. "I'm sure there are plenty of other examples of this."

Fry believes the ideas in her book would definitely be invaluable to a group or business that wants this sort of exposure. And I agree. She made a key point when she said that "people at the helm in such organizations know about fund-raising and promotion, but few know the magazine article-writing field."

But what about ideas? Where do you get them?

2. Ideas are everywhere.

For one thing, you don't invent them, according to Norman B. Rohrer, founding director of the Christian Writers Guild. "You recognize them."

"If you can't come up with an idea," observed Fry, "you just aren't paying attention."

How true!

Even so, Fry suggests the leaders of a nonprofit organization look to their membership and the work they've done—and the work and events they plan—for articles ideas.

3. Recycle current publications.

Chances are you already have some good material in your in-house newsletter. Have you thought of recycling it by sending it to another publication? Who knows, maybe one of your brochures can form the basis of a good article.

4. Address real problems.

If you're writing a tip sheet, think of a problem your group can solve. Think of the steps it would take for an individual to apply your suggestions. Then list those steps in chronological order.

For example:

▶ "7 Ways to Curb Teenage Drinking"
▶ "The Right Way to Help Abused Women"

Chances are you already have some good material in your in-house newsletter. Have you thought of recycling it by sending it to another publication?

- ▶ "10 Things You Should Know about Beating Cancer"
- ▶ "Quick Tips for Reaching Your Neighbors for Christ"

Each of those headlines promises benefits. In the trade, they're called "List" articles. Readers devour them, looking for tips to improve their lives or the lives of others.

5. Use colorful anecdotes.

Are you writing a general article?

"Most non-profits have countless anecdotes they can reference and events they can highlight in articles," noted Fry. "A non-profit organized around an illness, for example, might offer articles about the illness, famous people who are battling the illness or breakthroughs in a cure. Other ideas might focus on heart-warming stories of recovery, children with the illness, how people overcome the obstacles of the illness and different activities one can pursue with the illness and so forth," she said.

6. Use appropriate length.

When planning your article, it's a good idea to think about length. Generally speaking, editors will let you know how long the article should be. It may be anywhere from 700 to 2,500 words long.

Generally speaking, editors will let you know how long the article should be. It may be anywhere from 700 to 2,500 words long.

7. Study targeted periodicals.

Suppose you have a good idea. You have a treasure-trove of resources and you're now ready to write the article. What's next?

Review a copy of *Writer's Market*, which is published each year by Writer's Digest Books. The directory offers hundreds of listings for magazines (and book publishers) that use freelance articles. Another useful source is *The Literary Marketplace*. Of course, you may also do a search on the web.

8. Begin with a query.

"Always study the magazine first," advised Fry. "Next, submit a one-page query letter to the editor explaining your focus for this article. Do not send the completed article unless it is the magazine's policy to accept unsolicited manuscripts."

9. Prepare for rejection.

Following the above advice will enable you to place as many articles as you have time to write. Of course, that's in a best-case scenario. But in a worst case, "you won't hit the mark with any of the articles you pitch," Fry said.

"The range in between 'the two scenarios' is so wide," she said, "I can't even begin to predict the results. Someone writing for a specific audience and who has the expertise to write on that topic, will fare much better than those of us out here trying to be the 'be all.'"

10. Avoid blatant commercial copy.

A piece of advice that Fry offers to article writers is something worth framing and hanging on a wall. She said: "Make sure that you are offering the magazine something of value to their readers. That means no blatant promotional material, but a useful, informational, entertaining article."

Make writing and publishing a regular part of your campaign. Aim for the publication of one article each month. If some are rejected, revise them and resubmit, or send them to other periodicals. Continue with this practice, and you'll soon be reaching more people while enhancing your image as an authority in your field.

Make sure that you are offering the magazine something of value to their readers. That means no blatant promotional material, but a useful, informational, entertaining article.

Chapter 11

8 Proven Ways to Talk Your Way into the Limelight

How You Can Increase Your Exposure and Generate Income as a Public Speaker

PUBLIC SPEAKING IS TO A CAMPAIGN WHAT OIL IS TO AN ENGINE. Without it, you can turn the ignition, but you won't go very far.

Oral communication can be an organization's most effective and least expensive medium for transmitting information to the public," say the authors of *Public Relations*. "It may be informal, as in the casual exchange of ideas and opinions between management and employees at all levels; or it may be formal, as in addresses announced in advance and delivered to subordinates, shareholders, opinion leaders and the general public."

Because of the emphasis given to the press release (in this book and others), it is easy to focus on it at the expense of other publicity tools. But important as it is, a press release cannot take the place of a live person speaking before a hungry audience. A living, breathing, articulate, and compelling human being will always have an advantage when it comes to reaching your audience and generating coverage by the media.

There's no way around this fact. A speech can do things that simply cannot be done in print because some things are better heard than read. Think about Dr. Martin Luther King, Jr. Reading his speech is one thing, but hearing it is quite another. To make effective use of speaking as a promotional tool, there are primarily two factors to consider:

- **Your speaking ability:** Are you a good communicator? Do you have charisma? Are you lively and energetic? Can you hold an audience in a compelling way? Can you tell stories in an engaging manner? What about humor? Can you make people laugh? Do people applaud throughout your talks?

- **Advanced planning:** Have you done your homework? Have you taken the time to ensure that your slogan is a part of all of your communications? Do you have a list of topics that will appeal to your audience? Have you timed your engagements around other promotional activities? Can you work out the details with traveling and media coverage? Do you have someone who can assist you with administrative matters?

If you answered yes to each of the above questions, then you are ready to use public speaking as a marketing tool—and begin talking your way into the limelight. To get you started, I've listed eight important and highly practical tips that will give you a foundation for success. These tips are based on personal experiences and the insight of other professional speakers.

1. Develop a sample package.

This package should contain one or two CDs of your talks, as well as a query letter asking to speak for an upcoming event. Don't forget to include a photo, a list of topics you can address, and any background material that sheds light on your credentials and expertise. As you might have guessed, this package can be a press kit; but instead of being designed for news coverage, it's designed to secure a speaking engagement.

Your sample package should be mailed to meeting planners, conference organizers, or directors of various trade associations.

To ensure you've reached the right person, and to increase your chances of success, follow up within a week or so. Simply make a phone call and ask if your package was received and if more information is needed.

If calling on meeting planners is not your cup of tea, you can always advertise in speakers' bureau directories and have your name listed as an expert in media directories. According to Dottie Walters, purchasing ad

Your sample package should be mailed to meeting planners, conference organizers, or directors of various trade associations.

space in these publications is more cost-effective and less time-consuming than the use of direct mail to meeting planners.

2. Always notify the press.

Once you have a speaking engagement lined up, be sure to prepare advance press releases or a "media alert" announcing the subject, time, and place of the speech, together with biographical information. Then notify the press. Why? Because your appearances can be promoted as news events. "Whenever you speak, invite people to come and hear you—editors, producers, bureau representatives, potential clients," say Dottie and Lilly Walters. "Inviting people to preview you is excellent promotion."

To prevent duplication, in terms of contacting the press, you can ask the meeting planner if he or she plans to notify the press. If so, you can let them handle it. Or, you can prepare the material and give it to the meeting planner for submission to the press. This way, the press will get on the planner's letterhead. Submission from a third party will allow you to promote yourself without the appearance of being a selfish promoter.

The headline for your event might read:

- ▶ "Local author to speak at Lion's Club breakfast"
- ▶ "Local businesswoman to address high school students"
- ▶ "Young entrepreneur to address Chamber lunch crowd"
- ▶ "John Doe to speak at this year's fundraiser"

If you're fortunate enough to have a reporter attend your event, be prepared to provide him or her with a copy of your speech, along with your press kit.

If you're fortunate enough to have a reporter attend your event, be prepared to provide him or her with a copy of your speech, along with your press kit. Again, giving the reporter a hard copy of the speech will make his or her job easier. They won't have to take notes—and they will be more likely to "get it right" when quoting you.

In some cases, it's best to provide your speech at least a day in advance. This way, if the reporter cannot attend the event, he or she will still be able to write a story that's based on your talk.

Don't make the mistake I made while addressing a meeting sponsored by the Chamber of Commerce in Hanover, PA. At the end of the meeting, two reporters asked for a copy of my speech. Unfortunately, I only had one copy—the one that I used. Consequently, I had to decide which reporter would leave with the speech. Well, I made a choice. And now that I think about it, it was probably the wrong choice. Since this was before the age of e-mail, I couldn't send out a copy before the reporter's deadline. So I had to accept a large story in one paper and a tiny story in the other. Mind you, this was a mistake I'll never forget.

But what if the reporters do not attend your event? No problem. Simply write up a press release and submit it to the reporter along with your photo.

3. Collect names and letters of recommendation.

Without a good mailing list, your campaign will be limited. Without letters of recommendation, your credibility will be lacking and you will miss out on profitable speaking opportunities.

When your engagement is over, ask the meeting planner for a letter of recommendation. Such a letter will become a powerful tool for generating interest in your talks.

What to do? Use each of your engagements to collect the names of the attendees. One way to do this is to have a drawing for a free product or two. Ask the people in the audience to take a chance on receiving these great products by simply placing their business cards in the drawing box. A name is picked for the "prize" and you get to keep the rest of the names for your mailing list. Of course, you would need permission, and maybe assistance from the meeting planner in order to do this.

You can also bypass the "drawing box" idea and simply announce that your audience can receive a FREE copy of your newsletter. All they have to do is place their business cards in the box, or leave them with your assistant.

When your engagement is over, ask the meeting planner for a letter of recommendation. Such a letter will become a powerful tool for generating interest in your talks.

4. Record all of your talks.

When arranging to deliver a speech, ask the meeting planner if you can have the speech recorded. Video or audio would be fine. Doing this will enable you to develop products for future engagements. Before long, you could have a series of talks that you sell as an information package.

One speaker I know has his presentations recorded and then sends them out to prospects as premium incentives. Sometimes, when he's selling his books, he offers the recordings as a FREE bonus for "trying his product" and for ordering by a certain date.

Perhaps I should mention that a side benefit of having your talks recorded is that you can replay them for critiques and self-improvement. Review them with a critical eye or ear and make note of your weaknesses and your strong points. Use your findings to make the necessary changes. Practice and rehearse until you're the best you can be.

5. Arrange to speak at schools.

If your topic will appeal to a certain high school class, then contact the school principal and instructors. Inform them of how your talk will enlighten their students. For these engagements, chances are you will not be paid. Just remember to notify the media through a press release. If the school publishes a newspaper, ask to be featured.

If you wish to hit the college circuit (and you should), begin by contacting the professors of the classes for which you want to speak. Unlike the public high schools, the colleges/universities may offer you a fee for your service. But that's only one of the benefits. Another alternative is to teach continuing education courses for community colleges.

Speaking at colleges is more prestigious. When you can say in your promotions, "She has been a frequent lecturer at scores of colleges and universities, including Jane Doe University, John Doe Community College ...," your audience will be impressed.

6. Develop your own workshops and seminars.

During your presentation, be sure to give valuable information and not a sales pitch.

By now you can see that when it comes to speaking, you have many options. Another one you might consider is the development of your own workshops. You can do it the traditional way or use the electronic method.

With the traditional approach, you select a site, such as a hotel conference room, a library, or a meeting room at your place of business. Or, you could take a tip from the network marketers and hold the workshop in a spacious living room.

The workshop can be scheduled for evenings or a half-day, weekend session. You can promote it through ads and press releases. If this is your first, and you're not yet well-known, it may be best to promote it as a free event. Require participants to RSVP in order to ensure a seat.

During your presentation, be sure to give valuable information and not a sales pitch. At the end of your talk, you may encourage the participants to purchase your products. In this setting, it's a good idea to offer the products at discounts.

With the electronic method, you can take advantage of the Internet by offering "webinars"—seminars/workshops over the web. These web-based workshops are usually promoted by e-mail far in advance of the scheduled meeting. Most of them are free. Participants only need to sign up by e-mail, through which they're given an access code, and then visit the site at the designated time.

Another approach is the use of teleconferences. This is a favorite among entrepreneurs and independent marketers. As with the webinars, the conferences are promoted by e-mail, in which prospects are invited to call a certain phone number at a specific time. When they do, they get to hear interviews and presentations by various experts. They also have the privilege of asking questions.

As one would imagine, the electronic methods of holding workshops is more cost-effective than the traditional method. Of course, you don't always get to see the speakers, but you don't have to travel and bother with food and lodging issues. The cost is minimal, even for the long-distance phone calls during a teleconference.

If you choose to try the electronic method, it would help to first sample a few as a participant. This will allow you to see exactly how it works. You'll also get to see what you like and don't like about this method as a tool for your campaign.

7. Turn your talks into articles and books.

As I've suggested before, none of your talks should go to waste: They should be recycled in as many ways as possible.

Keep an updated list of the trade publications that feature articles on your topic. Contact these publications and ask to have your articles published.

Have you started a newsletter? Feature some of your talks as articles, along with an offer for the readers to order the audio or video version of the articles. You could write, for example, "If you enjoyed this article on how to _____ (fill in the blank), then you will love the audio version on CD that was delivered before _____ (fill in the blank). The cost is only $____. But if you order NOW, you pay only $_____—a savings of $_____."

Although articles are effective for self-promotion, they do not have the prestige of a published book. So as you review your speeches with the intent of turning them into other products, give the book your highest priority. Begin with a small booklet of 16 to 32 pages. If your schedule allows, you can start with a full-length publication that's 100 to 200 pages. If all of this seems daunting, it shouldn't. After all, you'll only need to compile the speeches you've already prepared, and then have them edited for a book format.

8. Become a "talking head" for the news media.

When the Oklahoma City bombing occurred, a smart college professor in Pennsylvania issued a media alert by fax to all of the local and regional

As you review your speeches with the intent of turning them into other products, give the book your highest priority.

media outlets. In his statement, he explained that he was an authority on terrorism and had done research on the type of tragedy that had occurred. He closed by saying he was available for comments or interviews about the tragedy in Oklahoma City.

Well, you can imagine how eager the reporters were to interview this local expert. I immediately called him and asked a few questions and began writing my story. The next day, I called him again for a follow-up story. During my interview with him, I asked about the other papers. He said his phone had been ringing off the hook for over 24 hours. When the dust had settled, this professor and his school had received coverage in scores of newspapers. They were also featured on numerous television news programs. All of this happened because an alert observer was following the news and he seized the moment to let the media know he was available.

The same could happen to you. In fact, you don't have to wait for a major tragedy or breaking news. You may contact the media in advance and let them know who you are. Encourage them to contact you when they need an expert opinion. Believe me, when the need arises, they will call.

In practically every newsroom I have worked in, the editor kept a listing of various experts who could be called in a moment's notice. Each time a major story broke, this listing was used by every reporter who was working on the story.

Now It's Your Turn

If you apply the tips outlined above, you can expect to see an increase in visibility, extra income, and coverage by the news media. Public speaking can be one of the most personable and exciting experiences you will have as a business professional.

Do what you can to make it a key component of your current—and all future—promotional campaigns. And, as the saying goes, don't stop until the fat lady sings.

Chapter 12

7 Tips for Writing a Column for Magazines, Newsletters, or Your Local Newspaper

How to Become a Sought-After Expert on a Local, Regional, or National Level

H AVE YOU TRIED USING A COLUMN TO PROMOTE YOUR BUSINESS? Take a look at your local newspapers—the big ones and the little ones. Flip through a few pages and see how many columns are used. How many are written by people like you? Or your competitors?

Depending on where you live, you might see only a few. And that's a shame. Why? Because newspapers are in need of quality material. And finding it is not always easy. However, by skimping out in this area of writing, a business will undoubtedly miss out on a grand opportunity.

It's Better Than a Press Release

Unlike the press release which may or may not be published ... or the feature article, which may find print, but on a sporadic basis ... a column—in your local newspaper—is a powerful outlet for reaching a select audience on a regular basis. It is a guaranteed route to visibility and a proven way to be remembered.

The suggestions I'll make here will apply to any organization—commercial or nonprofit—on a local level. In such a case, the local paper is a crucial tool for establishing a presence and for reaching prospects. However, the principles for writing a column may still be adapted by companies with a national audience. Instead of local papers, however, these companies would benefit by seeking out regional and national publications.

Before beginning your column, you must first define your objectives. Next, you have to identify your resources. From there, determine the kind of column that will best meet your needs.

Different Types of Columns

When you're ready to write a column, you have many ways in which to write it. Here are some possible approaches.

Commentary: Has your organization taken a stand on a hot political issue? Do you have strong feelings about a certain danger? Are you aware of certain fears in your community that need to be addressed? If you answered yes to any of these questions, you might consider writing a commentary in which you explain the problems and offer solutions.

Invite readers to send you questions by regular mail or e-mail. Use them as the basis for your column.

Question-and-Answer: Invite readers to send you questions by regular mail or e-mail. Use them as the basis for your column. If you have a striking theme, the Q&A approach can be very effective. If nothing else, it will compel people to read your work just to see their questions in print. They might even clip out the columns and share them with family and friends. Some readers, no doubt, will become loyal clients, customers, and even fans.

Straight news: A news column works best if your company is busy making news. But let's suppose you aren't making any news—on a weekly basis. What then?

Cull news items from other sources that relate to your product or service. Depending on how your news is gathered, you may need to get permission for publication. But whether it's required or not, it's a good policy to always credit sources. Your goal is to keep readers thinking about your business and its related activities. A good resource for newsy items is the Internet. Get on a few mailing lists. Sign up for free e-newsletters. Then, like an old-timer mining for gold, extract the good stuff and weave it into your column.

Instructional: One of the most popular columns you can write is the one loaded with how-to information. It's also my personal favorite and one I find incredibly easy to write. Some time ago, when I asked a friend (an internist) about writing a weekly column offering tips and ideas about certain heath-care issues, he gasped.

"Are you kidding?" he asked me. "I'm no writer. Where would I get the ideas?"

Smiling, I pointed to the stack of pamphlets in his waiting room.

"Surely, you can borrow some of this," I said. "Or write about the most common questions you hear from patients."

He got the message and went away smiling. I later showed him how to recycle the work in his small newsletter. We looked at how he could repackage it for a wider audience.

Time-Tested Tips for Writing a Good Column

Below are a few fundamentals to keep in mind when writing a column. They should prove helpful whether you write for a penny shopper, a small weekly, or a mid-sized daily newspaper.

1. Use engaging headlines.

Some editors are picky when it comes to headlines in newspapers. You may submit a suggested headline, but nine times out of ten, it will be changed. That's because editors have different tastes and a certain amount of space to fill.

Then too, a column headline can take on one form in a newspaper and another in a magazine. For instance, a magazine might use an instructional head like: "10 Tips for Keeping Your Pet Warm in the Winter." In a newspaper, the headline will likely have a newsy form, like: "Local doctor offers warnings about pets in the cold." I suggest you experiment. But first, study the style of the publication in which your column will appear. You want your work to be different and to stand out from the rest. But not so different that it clashes with the editor's overall package.

You want your work to be different and to stand out from the rest. But not so different that it clashes with the editor's overall package.

2. Make it relevant and client-centered.

As with any promotional document, you make your copy relevant by engaging readers, and by showing how they are affected by your information. In a sense, you have to put on your marketing cap and ask, "What's in for *them*? Why should they care?

Demonstrate the importance of your work by mentioning names of actual people. Draw on case studies and recent news reports that relate to your subject. Write in such a way that the reader will think, "Wow, that's pretty close to home."

If you're writing about crime and you want to rally support, then pour on the fear. You may mention statistics, but as everyone knows, it takes a face—actual people—to drive the point home.

If need be, use your own personal story to illustrate the urgency of the moment.

3. Make it friendly.

A friendly column is personable, chatty, and entertaining. It uses no strong-arm tactics or hard-sell language. After all, it's not a direct mail piece.

A friendly column has the feel of a personal letter, but unlike fundraising letters, it is less direct in asking for support. In most cases, it will not ask for any support. Its purpose is to inform in a nonthreatening way.

It may certainly have direct response elements and triggers, but in a subtle way. Anything more is the equivalent of a TV infomercial, something that can hurt your credibility—with editors and readers.

A friendly column has the feel of a personal letter, but unlike fundraising letters, it is less direct in asking for support.

To make your column friendly, pretend you're writing a letter to a close friend (I know, you hear this all the time). Use short and simple words. Vary the length of paragraphs and sentences. Pepper your work with contractions. Use images and ideas that your readers can relate to. Try not to speak over the reader's head.

4. Watch out for jargon.

When writing for an in-house publication, you can use certain jargon that will be easily understood. But when writing for a general audience—the kind who reads newspapers—you must hold back on the industry jargon, unless, of course, you can explain it.

Special care must be taken to ensure your work doesn't read like the minutes of a board meeting. Spruce it up with a powerful lead paragraph. Keep it organized. Then close with a bang.

5. Make it lively—tell a good story.

Ideally, you can open with a dramatic, startling statement that stops readers in their tracks. Example: "A major league baseball player has withdrawn his support for the local soup kitchen."

You can also open with a compelling story or anecdote, something that will hook readers, pique their curiosity, or build suspense.

Example: "It was 11:35 p.m. when I drove by the house and saw 11-year-old Brandon kneeling by the car. He had a white cap in his hand. I stopped and blew my horn, but he ignored me. When I stepped out of the car ...."

6. Mix it up with different literary forms.

Another thing worth trying is to mix up certain forms. By this, I mean, use stories in some, offer news in some, and sprinkle a little history in others. At times, you may include stories, news, and history all wrapped up in a single column.

7. Include a Resource Box.

The Resource Box is that "box" of information at the end of a column that tells the reader who you are and how they can benefit from your service or products. It includes all necessary contact information: phone number, e-mail address, web site.

Yet, to make it work as a direct response tool, the box also should have an offer. Free booklets, brochures, and newsletters all make for good offers. Unfortunately, many writers settle for bloated copy about their organization or about themselves. They stop there without bothering to trigger a response from the reader.

At times, you may include stories, news, and history all wrapped up in a single column.

A model Resource Box

Take a cue from Ann Landers. At the bottom of her syndicated column, you'll find offers for booklets she's written. Here's one I saw some time ago:

"What can you give the person who has everything? Ann Landers' booklet, 'Gems,' is ideal for nightstand or coffee table. 'Gems' is a collection of Ann Landers' most requested poems and essays. Send a self-addressed, long, business-size envelope and a check or money order for $5.25 (this includes postage and handling) to: Gems, in care of Ann Landers, P.O. Box 11562, Chicago, Ill. 60611-0562. To find out more about Ann Landers and read her past columns, visit the Creators Syndicate web page at www.creators.com."

This Resource Box does all the right things, in terms of marketing. If I were to change something, I would probably shorten it a bit. In fact, some editors do not include the section because it adds about three to four inches to the column. Still, it's a good model, even if you're not selling your offer.

Think of something you or your business can offer readers. Then try, in as few words as possible, to model your Resource Box after the one used by Ann Landers.

Always Think Ahead

Before committing yourself to writing a column, be sure to keep an idea file. Whenever an idea strikes you, jot it down and file it away. Always think ahead and keep your idea file full. In the best of circumstances, you'll have enough material to keep you busy for at least a year or more.

Chapter 13

12 Things You Should Know About Writing and Publishing Books

How to Use a Book or Booklet as the Ultimate Marketing Tool

WHEN THE GREAT DAVID OGILVY WANTED TO PROMOTE HIS AD agency, he wrote a book titled, *Confessions of an Advertising Man*. The book quickly became a hit. In addition to positioning Ogilvy as a leading authority on advertising, it was instrumental in attracting clients for Ogilvy's ad agency.

When pioneer copywriter Maxwell Sackheim wanted to increase his client list, he ran a full-page ad in the April 29, 1952 issue of *The New York Times*. The ad used the headline, "Seven Deadly Advertising Mistakes." "While it may seem at first glance to be violently negative in its appeal, the ad brought in requests for more than 10,000 copies of its contents in booklet form, from all over the world," Sackheim recalled. "Those who responded included advertising professionals, students, college professors, and others not remotely connected with the advertising business," Sackheim said.

These two cases illustrate the possibilities that lie in writing a book, be it large or small. Besides generating money through actual sales, a book can be used as a marketing tool to promote businesses and generate leads.

Throughout history, books have been used to accomplish many feats in society. Thomas Paine wrote *Common Sense*, a booklet that fired up the American Revolution. Harriet Beecher Stowe's book, *Uncle Tom's Cabin*, gave voice to slaves and supported the movement to bring slavery to an end. Perhaps you can name other titles that affected history in a profound way. Better yet, you could probably name a few titles that affected you or your business in a profound way.

12 Things You Should Know About Using Books

If you're planning a promotional campaign with the hopes of getting media coverage that will boost the sales of your products or services, then it will help you to know more about books and the advantages of being an author. For this reason, I want to share with you 12 things you should know about using books as a marketing tool in your campaign.

Because of the news value of a published book, an author has instant media attraction.

1. A book has good press appeal.

A retailer can hardly hope to get press coverage for a new bicycle or other products on the shelf. Unless a real estate agent can do something that's significantly newsworthy or earth-shattering, she cannot expect coverage. This is not so with an author. Because of the news value of a published book, an author has instant media attraction. In fact, a book is one of the few products that will pique the interest of a reporter. The better the book, the greater your chances of being covered. If what you write strikes a cord with the media's audience, and it offers valuable, useful information, you can count on the media taking notice.

2. A book will showcase all of your credentials.

As an author, your book will speak for you. Even when you're at home relaxing, it will circulate your credentials before an interested audience, including prospects, clients, and employers. Here's how it is done.

Most books have an "About the Author" section that provides information on the writer's background. You can use this section as a modified resume or vitae. Be bold and toot your own horn. This is not the place to be shy. Highlight your strong points and your best achievements. Include everything that will portray you as an expert. Write up a full page or two, and include your photograph along with contact information. Go a step farther and include a "bio blurb" on the back cover. By making your resume a part of your publication, you're able to promote yourself each time a book is sold or distributed.

3. A book will help position you in the marketplace.

A book is a sure-fire way to become known as an expert. Think of all the experts and widely publicized leaders in your field. How did you come to know them? Chances are, it was through their books, or a forum provided as a result of their books. Perhaps you saw them on TV being interviewed about their books. Or you heard a lecture that was based on their books. Maybe you read their newsletter designed to promote their books. Or someone recommended them ... because of their books.

So you see? A book is the perfect springboard for taking your promotions to a higher level. "Once your book is published, your status as an expert becomes permanent," say the authors of *Guerrilla Publicity*. "It can never be taken away. You're listed in the Library of Congress, in the Copyright Office, and with Amazon.com."

4. A book will demonstrate your talent and tenacity.

Writing a book is not only a demonstration of your knowledge as an expert, but your skill as a writer and communicator. It also shows you have the discipline and talent to see a project through. Let's face it. Many people dream of writing a book and many talk of doing it. Yet, they never get around to doing it. But not you. As an author, you will have proven yourself and earned a title that you can keep for life. In the eyes of many, including the press, it's a feat worthy of attention, and in some cases, lots of respect.

5. A book can be a source of extra income.

Some books make lots of money and some do not. For some authors, the financial gains are made directly from the sale of the books; but for most authors, books are used to help propel their careers. While bestseller status is something to be desired (and something you should definitely work toward), for most businesspeople, it is more practical to use the book as a promotional tool that can lead to income from other sources. Obviously you

Writing a book is not only a demonstration of your knowledge as an expert, but your skill as a writer and communicator.

should work hard to promote your book and sell what you can with the hopes of making a profit. But keep an eye on the benefits you can receive through other sources because of the book.

6. It offers benefits for the present and future.

Unlike any other tool you may use, a book will serve you well on both a short-term and long-term basis.

The fact is, a book can play a major role in your public relations campaign. Unlike any other tool you may use, a book will serve you well on both a short-term and long-term basis. Among other things, it can spur interest in your current campaign and continue to move people long after your campaign has ended. You actually get more than 15 minutes of fame.

Joe Vitale is fond of saying that a book will give you immortality. The reason is that it lives on long after you are gone. Now think about it. Even in death, your obituary will mention you as an author, thereby allowing you to promote from the grave. This cannot be said of most other products.

7. A book is an effective tool for networking and name-dropping.

Your book is an ideal source for dropping the names of the people you know and respect. It is a place to pay homage to friends, colleagues, experts, and celebrities. How is this done? In addition to being sprinkled throughout the book, their names can be listed (or even highlighted) in the Acknowledgments section of your publication. You could also feature important names on the Dedication page. Keep in mind, when you take these steps to recognize others, they will likely return the favor in some form or another. Just remember to send them a copy of the book when it is published.

8. A book can be used as a mini-catalog.

Dr. Jeffrey Lant took this practice to a new level and found much success. At the back of all of his books, he included his full catalog that promoted his products and services. His products included books, special reports, and tapes/CDs. His services included consulting, speaking engagements, and copywriting. Of course, he always included a strong, compelling call to action.

You can follow his example by including your other products and services in your book. This way, each time a reader holds your book, he or she is invited to try your other offerings.

9. A book can be used to generate leads.

Your book can be given freely to prospects as a premium incentive to try your product or service. It's one of the most effective ways to generate interest in what you have to offer.

When I wanted to generate leads for my copywriting service, I wrote a single-page letter that offered a free copy of my booklet, "Trigger Phrases that Make People Act—NOW!" I mailed this to prospects and received many replies. It resulted in many assignments.

What about your campaign? How about writing a small booklet or pamphlet that gives useful how-to information related to your business? Offer it as a FREE bonus to those who respond by a certain date. Remind the readers that this is a limited offer and will not be repeated. Or you could say that a free copy will be rushed to the first 50 people who respond.

10. A book can be used to close deals.

If you're competing for a contract and you're the only author in the running, a book will tip the scales in your favor. I know this from personal experience.

When I learned of an organization that wanted to raise money for a World War II project, I contacted the director and included my book, *Off to War: Franklin Countians in World War II*. After reviewing the book and samples of my work, the director called me and made an offer. When I completed my first assignment, I was given another one almost immediately. In no uncertain terms, the book had made the difference, as it showed I had an understanding of WWII issues.

If you're competing for a contract and you're the only author in the running, a book will tip the scales in your favor.

11. It can be used to acquire speaking engagements.

In 1998, I began holding workshops for state press associations because of a manual I'd self-published on journalism. It was called, *Scooping the Competition: How to be FIRST in Reporting Hot Stories* and was printed as a 132-page guide (comb-bound) at the local Mail Boxes Etc. When the directors of the associations learned about my book, they called me and asked what I would charge to do a workshop. They offered to cover travel and other expenses in addition to my fee. They also agreed to promote the manual and assist me in selling it at my workshops.

Elated, I accepted all of the invitations and then used the contacts I had made to secure other engagements. Although the manual was never released by a traditional publisher, it opened doors for me that resulted in thousands of dollars in extra income.

12. It can be used to spin off series of other products.

"If you can sell your information one way, you can usually sell it, with modifications, most of the other ways," says Gordon Burgett.

I call this "recycling." As such, your book can be repackaged as speeches, workshops, articles, CDs, special reports, or the content for a newsletter. Even more, it can become the foundation of a series of books (think of Jay Levinson and his *Guerilla* series).

All it takes is a little creativity. Begin by analyzing each chapter. Perhaps one chapter can be used as a speech. Another one may be used as an article for a magazine or newsletter. Another one can be marketed as a special report. Maybe one can be used as a tip sheet and then offered as a free bonus. Just use your imagination.

If you hit the speaking circuit, it is necessary to have multiple products in order to be financially successful. Ideally, you want to offer package deals.

If you hit the speaking circuit, it is necessary to have multiple products in order to be financially successful. Ideally, you want to offer package deals. Example: A book combined with a special report, CDs, and a newsletter. Combining the products allows you to charge more—and sell more—at any given time. Of course, you could move prospects to action by offering them a special discount when they purchase "a set" or "the package." Explain the savings. "If you purchased each of these separately, it would cost you _____. But purchase them as a package and you only pay _____. That's a savings of _____."

Get the picture?

How To Strengthen Your Book And Make It More Marketable

If your book is to make a good impression and sell in today's demanding market, it has to be strong. That is, it must be properly packaged and bear the marks of a professional product. Below are five things you can do to strengthen your book and make it more salable—and useful as a marketing tool.

Highlight your credentials: When readers pick up your book, do they know from a glance they are dealing with an expert? One way to convince them is by highlighting your credentials—and doing it up front. It's like introducing a speaker. You wouldn't note the credentials at the end of the speech. Rather, you do it *before* the talk to build trust and anticipation with the listeners.

With a book, you can start on the front cover. State the title of the book and your name with professional title or accomplishment. Example: "... by

Jane Doe, the woman who has helped millions lose weight." You could mention the author's name and the title of other books the author has written. Example: "... by John Doe, the bestselling author of *Write Your Own Book*." You also may use both the author's title and name of other books. Example: "... by Mary Doe, Senator John Doe's Campaign Manager, and author of *How to Talk and be Heard*."

After the front cover, the next useful location is the back cover. There you can give a brief bio and blurbs, along with details about the benefits inside.

Support your claims: Today, it's not enough to simply make a claim in your writing. You must support it. One way to support your claim is by quoting credible sources. You further strengthen your position, use statistics, testimonials, case histories, and personal anecdotes.

"There are two ways of establishing a proposition," said Abe Lincoln. "One is by trying to demonstrate it upon reason; and the other is, to show that great [people] in former times have thought so and so, and thus to pass it by the weight of pure authority."

Few people can make strong claims that will stand without quoting others. The president of the United States can state his position, but even he will quote past presidents and poets.

Credit your sources: "Your book doesn't have to resemble a term paper to be of professional quality. But, depending on your subject, it should include reference notes, footnotes, a bibliography, or other methods of documentation for sources cited. When you credit your sources, you show courtesy and good scholarship. You bring recognition to the sources while introducing your readers to other experts.

This is where some books fail. And some, unfortunately, border on plagiarism. "Conventionally, the professional writer commands his words and those of others, but he never implies he owns the words of others," wrote Ken Macrorie in *Writing to Be Read*.

While using quotes is certainly a key element in sprucing up your book, you don't have to go overboard in noting where you got them. "Credit should naturally be given for every quotation, but there is no need to be overcome by gratitude," wrote Jacques Barzun and Henry F. Graff in *The Modern Researcher*.

Make it reader-friendly: Good books are easy to read and easy to use. You can improve yours by including a glossary, checklist, or index, where appropriate. Speak in familiar terms. Be specific. Use shorthand, long sentences, with plenty of subheads. For added strength include anecdotes and visual

While using quotes is certainly a key element in sprucing up your book, you don't have to go overboard in noting where you got them.

graphics. They can bring a dead book to life. Besides giving a touch of entertainment—and breathing space—they break up the fuzziness in your work and help drive points home.

Use a good proofreader: When it comes to hiring a proofreader, you won't save money by doing it yourself. Unless you are perfect (and most of us are not), you may actually lose money, not to mention your pride, when you spot embarrassing typos that crept into your finished book. So before you visit the typesetter or printer, be sure to use a good proofreader.

Put these tips to work and see if they won't make your book stronger, more marketable, and a powerful promotional tool for your campaign.

How to Get Your Book Published

Getting a book published today is a real challenge that requires skills, talent, salesmanship, and lots of perseverance.

Getting a book published today is a real challenge that requires skills, talent, salesmanship, and lots of perseverance. It's common knowledge that most of the major publishers today will not accept queries or proposals directly from writers; they prefer, instead, to accept submissions through literary agents. This is usually not the case with small publishers, who prefer to work directly with writers. Of course you can self-publish and skip the submission process altogether. But in doing so, you take responsibility of all the expenses—and all the risks.

Whether you choose to approach agents, big publishers, or small publishers, you must approach them the same way. This is first by query (sales letter to pitch your idea). If they like your query, they will ask to see a proposal (details below). If they like the proposal, they will offer a contract and sometimes an advance payment against royalties. At this point, you are usually given about six months to a year to complete the book.

Below are a few pointers for contacting publishers and/or agents.

Select the right publisher.

There are a number of guides available that will help you find publishers. The most popular are: *Writer's Market*, *The Literary Marketplace*, and *The International Directory of Small Publishers and Magazines*. Other ways to locate publishers is by visiting the library or bookstore (or Amazon.com). Simply find the books that are similar to yours or those that deal with your topic. Then make note of the publisher. In some cases, by reading the acknowledgments, you'll find the names of editors who worked on the book, as wells as the agent who sold it.

Begin with a one-page query letter.

This is actually a sales letter used to pitch your idea. Summarize what your book is about, how long it will be, competing books, your credentials, etc. Offer to provide a proposal, which is usually the second step of the process.

The proposal may be anywhere from 5 to 20 pages.

The proposal should contain all of the following information:

▶ **An overview of the book:** This could be done in a couple of paragraphs.

▶ **The market or audience for the book:** Identify the people who will buy your book. Note the size of the market. Quote statistics.

▶ **A list of competing books currently on the market:** List three or four titles that may compete with yours.

▶ **The uniqueness of your book:** Explain or show how your book is different.

▶ **Your bio sheet/resume/credentials, etc.:** Write one page showing how you are qualified to write the book. Show yourself as an authority.

▶ **Your plans for marketing or promoting the book:** List such things as speaking engagements, e-mail/Internet campaign, book reviews, etc.

▶ **Table of contents:** Here you list the title and subtitles of the book's chapters.

▶ **The format:** List the number of pages, pictures/graphics, and when it will be completed.

▶ **An annotated chapter-by-chapter outline of the book.**

▶ **Two or three sample chapters.**

The Internet is full of info on how to write query letters and book proposals. Do a search. Three resources are www.writers.net, www.about.com, and www.bly.com. Also, most book publishers have their submission guidelines posted on their web sites. Or you may write to request them. If you want to try your hand at self-publishing, I recommend *The Self-Publishing Manual* by Dan Poynter and *The Complete Guide to Self-Publishing* by Marilyn and Tom Ross. You would also benefit from John Kremer's *1001 Ways to Market Your Book*.

With a published book under your belt, you can tell everyone you meet that you're an author. Be prepared to give the title and where it can be purchased. If you're lucky, word of your achievement will catch wings and spread in many directions.

The Internet is full of info on how to write query letters and book proposals. Do a search.

Chapter 14

12 Cost-Cutting Ideas for Promoting Your Message with Postcards

How to Generate Publicity for Pennies on the Dollar

YOU'VE HEARD OF PEOPLE RECEIVING MAIL THAT WAS SO ENTICING, they couldn't put it down. They were immediately gripped by the copy on the outer envelope and lured inside to see what was offered. But what about mail that is so compelling, people snatch it out of a trash can? And they do it in public, in the presence of strangers and friends. Ever hear of it?

I saw such an act once during the final days of the presidential campaigns of 2000. The Republicans in Pennsylvania pulled out all the stops, using ads, press releases, faxes, speeches, and postcards to drive their message home.

When I walked into the post office one day, I saw a few of their postcards on the floor. I picked them up and was moving toward a table when I saw a couple of people reaching into the trash.

Had they dropped something? Perhaps their own mail ... by accident?

No. They were reaching for a postcard. Whether they were Democrats or Republicans, I don't know. But one thing is for sure, they were so taken by the message on the card, they were shameless about retrieving it from the trash.

I walked away with a big smile on my face, feeling envious of the person who designed those postcards. As I thought about the situation, it occurred to me that postcards are still a viable means of communication.

Postcards Have Many Advantages

Despite their potential, however, they are rarely used by many businesses. With the exception of political candidates, few ever dream of adding postcards to their campaigns.

It is certainly true that postcards will not work for everyone. But the same can be said of other fundraising tools. While the cards will not have the weight or power of a full direct mail package or newsletter, they can carry their weight—and do it well—when properly used.

"Postcards are a standard format for vacationers writing to relatives and for the response side of direct marketing, but not too many advertisers use them as direct mail," notes Mark S. Bacon in *Do-It-Yourself Direct Marketing*. "The advantages of postcards are their shorter lead times and low production costs compared to other formats. Since they are relatively scarce in advertising, their uniqueness makes them stand out."

While the cards will not have the weight or power of a full direct mail package or newsletter, they can carry their weight—and do it well—when properly used.

Effective Uses of Postcards

Postcards are ideal for a number of reasons. Like self-mailers, they have the power to create awareness-building impressions for your organization or cause. Mark S. Bacon rightly observes that "with the right creative idea, a postcard can have the attention-grabbing power of a much larger or elaborate mailing piece."

Consider using postcards for:

1. Friendly reminders

Has a prospect failed to respond? Send a reminder. Do you have an upcoming event and you'd like to boost attendance? Send a card. The card also works with the press. Perhaps you've requested their presence at a fundraiser and you want to make sure they attend. Again, send a card.

2. Breaking news

Have some late-breaking news? Have you had a crisis? An emergency? Use postcards to alert your customers. If you're in politics and your opponent has slammed you, fight back ... counter quickly ... through postcards.

3. Collector's item

Some cards are collector's items. They're designed to be kept and praised. They're perfect mementos. At the same time, they can create a lasting awareness of your business. To work, however, they must have a striking picture—drawing, painting, or photograph. Something worth saving. What would help? The works of a famous artist or photographer. "The old-fashioned picture postcard is a theme you can use to your advantage," writes Chuck Green in the article, "Rethinking Post Cards" (www.desktoppub.about.com). "This design plays on what you expect a postcard to be. But what looks like a souvenir from a museum is actually an announcement from a restaurant. A painting by the Impressionist Monet graces one side, the message, set in elegant type, is opposite."

4. Mini-newsletters

If it impacts your promotional efforts, and you need to get the word out quickly, you may use the postcard as a "special bulletin."

In some cases, your cards can work overtime like a mini-newsletter. Something happens and you want your audience to be the first to know about it. Instead of waiting for the quarterly newsletter, you send the information within days of the event. Maybe a celebrity has agreed to endorse your product. Maybe a building permit has been canceled. Or perhaps a key player in your company has resigned. Whatever the case, if it impacts your promotional efforts, and you need to get the word out quickly, you may use the postcard as a "special bulletin."

Obviously, where issues are too sensitive for the general public, discretion must be used. In such a case, an open, self-mailed postcard would not be the tool of choice.

5. Thank you notes

In an article titled "Thank Your Donors," (www.nonprofit.about.com), writer Stan Hutton points out the strength of using postcards. "Now that we've entered the world of e-mail, receiving a handwritten letter is almost as rare as finding a four-leaf clover," he says. "So imagine the impact when your donor finds a short thank you note written in your hand in his or her mailbox. You only need to jot down a few lines. What you say is less important than how you say it."

If you're short on staff or have lots of thank-you's to send out, he says, "a postcard is better than nothing. It acknowledges the gift and, if nothing else, lets the donor know that the check arrived in the mail."

6. Special offers

Customers and clients like to feel appreciated, as do most people. As you develop incentives and gifts to offer them as tokens of appreciation, promote your offers with postcards. Include pictures of the gift. Some religious groups have made the practice an art form. Whether they're offering coins, pendants or books, they showcase the item using colorful photographs that seem to leap off the card.

As you develop incentives and gifts to offer them as tokens of appreciation, promote your offers with postcards.

7. Famous quotes

Famed writer and humorist, Mark Twain, who thrived on self-promotion, used postcards to promote his work. A set of his cards were found after his death, which allowed him to promote his name, as it were, even from the grave. Twain's postcards were known for their quotes. Here are some examples:

- ▶ "Truth is the most valuable thing we have. Let us economize it."
- ▶ "Noise proves nothing. Often a hen who has merely laid an egg cackles as if she had laid an asteroid."
- ▶ "When in doubt tell the truth."
- ▶ "A man with a new idea is a crank until the idea succeeds."
- ▶ "Nothing so needs reforming as other people's habits."

Now, think of your cause, your business. What messages would you like to instill in your supporters? How often would you like to send those messages?

8. Compelling images

When you begin to write copy for your postcard, consider the space you have available. Depending on the size of your card, you may have room for a picture and headline on one side (the billboard side), and your message on the other, along with mailing address (response section).

Some cards work well without pictures or drawings. Like a powerful ad, they work on the strength of their copy. Of course, your goals will determine the format you choose.

9. Space ads

Think of the postcard as a two-sided space ad, where every word must count or be cut. Open with a strong headline, a grabber. Use a statement or question that will shock the reader.

10. Teasers

One side of the card may be viewed as the outer envelope of a direct mail package: Use teaser copy to draw the reader. If done right, it should prompt the reader to turn the card over for more information.

Another idea for moving the reader is to pique his or her curiosity by using an incomplete statement. Such a point was driven home recently by Ilise Benum in her newsletter, *Quick Online Marketing Tip* (www.artofself-promotion.com). Her advice was aimed at marketers on the Internet. She told them to start their messages in the subject line of their e-mail.

"People decide whether to delete an e-mail message based on who it's from and what's in the subject line," she said. "Instead of summarizing the content of the message in your subject line, try starting your message there and then continuing in the actual message box."

Benum gave this example, which would also work with postcards:

An editor sent her a message with the following subject line, "I like your ideas, but we have a teensy problem ..."

Great teaser, don't you think?

Use teaser copy to draw the reader. If done right, it should prompt the reader to turn the card over for more information.

11. Bells and whistles

Other elements worth trying are the bells and whistles. You know, the bullets, bursts, lines, arrows, etc. Don't hesitate to pour them on. You have only a little space and a short amount of time to grab readers and move them to action. For this reason, you must rely on any eye-catcher that will work.

If need be, bring on the bold type. Underline key phrases. Highlight important words. Draw circles around important sentences. Scribble notes in the margins. Do what's necessary to stop readers in their tracks.

12. Call to action

Always include some kind of call to action. Give deadlines where appropriate. Highlight premium incentives.

Once you have your complete message delivered in a compact, but vibrant manner, go to work on the other essentials. Order blank and contact information. If you have a web site, include it. Working like a brochure (or media kit) like this answers questions. It also gives the reluctant prospects another incentive to respond. If you're lucky, you might create a postcard like the one mentioned above. If for some reason it lands in the trash bin, it will be so compelling that people will pull it out. They will salvage it and do exactly what you want them to do—RESPOND!

Chapter 15

7 Exciting Tips for Collecting and Using Good Testimonials

Easy Ways to Establish Credibility in the Eyes of Your Prospects and Customers

T*ESTIMONIALS ARE AN EFFECTIVE METHOD OF FREE PROMOTION, SIM-*ply because people are interested in the comments and reactions of other people," says marketing expert Ted Nicholas. "Endorsement of a product by one person tends to lower the natural sales resistance of another."

Nicholas, who has made millions of dollars through his self-promotional campaigns, points out the fact that people generally are more likely to be interested in a product which other people make favorable comments about.

Now armed with this knowledge, you can be on the lookout for good testimonials. Where they don't exist, you can ask for them. Sometimes they will arrive unexpectedly and unsolicited. At times, you may spot them in discussion groups, on Amazon.com, or in articles published in the print media. How or where you find them is not all that important; it's the habit of using them that will make the difference in your campaign.

What follows is a list of important tips for collecting and using testimonials in your campaign.

1. Testimonials may be collected from customers, clients, colleagues, experts, and celebrities.

It would be great to receive testimonials from celebrities, but for your local campaign, it might be better to use an endorsement from a local name that's respected in your community. If you aim to reach people on a regional level, it would help to have names recognized by that region.

While name recognition will certainly help, testimonials from satisfied customers will likely be your best endorsements—and the shining proof of your quality of service. Where possible, try to use the full names in your communications.

Sometimes you see ads with great testimonials that are signed by "N.H., New Jersey." I call this, "nameless people." Even though initials are better than nothing at all, it is far better to use actual names. When you begin collecting endorsements, it's OK to be creative and candid. Over the years, I've found a number of retailers who distribute "Tell us what you think" cards. They hand these cards to all customers whenever they make purchases. Sometimes they offer a discount or FREE bonus for responding. This is a proven way to collect testimonials.

If you're in dire need of an expert endorsement, locate one in your field and provide him or her with a complimentary product or service. Then ask for their opinion and if they would recommend what you're offering.

An excellent resource for reaching celebrities is Jordan McAuley's e-zine, "Contact Any Celebrity News" (http://contactanycelebrity.com). You may also want to order a copy of John Kremer's e-book, "Blurbs for Your Books: How to Get High-Profile Testimonials from Celebrities and Other Notable VIPs" (MegaNiche Media, www.meganiche.com).

Testimonials from satisfied customers will likely be your best endorsements— and the shining proof of your quality of service.

2. The best testimonials are specific about certain benefits.

If a customer says, "I really like your service," that's fine. But it would be better for them to say specifically what they like about your service. If you receive such a comment (and I'm certain you will), it is OK to write them and ask for more details. Example:

"Mr. Doe, we were delighted to receive your letter and to learn of your satisfaction with our service. Your kind words are always appreciated.

"However, since we're constantly updating our equipment and seeking ways to improve our service, I was wondering if you would mind sharing what you like about our business, and why.

"I have enclosed a self-addressed stamped envelope for your convenience. Again, thank you so much for taking the time to share with us."

3. Seek permission in writing before publishing.

When a customer or client provides you with a compelling endorsement, always thank them and immediately ask for their permission to use it in your promotional campaign. This will help you to avoid embarrassment and potential legal hassles.

Advise them that their words may appear in ads, books, newsletters, on your web site, and in other documents. To save time and encourage good cooperation, simply write up a permission form in advance and ask the customer or client to sign it.

Since you will always be on the lookout for testimonials, this practice should become an automatic feature of your campaign.

Since you will always be on the lookout for testimonials, this practice should become an automatic feature of your campaign. I saw an example of this recently when I contacted a well-known author to thank him for his work and the impact he'd had on my writing. I did it via a short e-mail.

Within minutes, he wrote back. After thanking me for my comments, he asked if he could use my words on his web site. I eagerly gave him permission to use my comments in any or all of his promotional documents.

4. They should be used on most promotional documents.

When creating your marketing pieces, always leave space for one or more testimonials. As noted earlier, testimonials can be used in letters, brochures, advertisements, web sites, press releases, postcards, and newsletters.

Use the best ones for headlines. For others, you can highlight them with compelling graphics by placing them in boxes (or borders), using large or bold type, or using a striking color like red.

When you have collected a large number, consider using a full page (front and back) with nothing but testimonials. The heading could say, "What they say about Jane Doe and her services..."

This page of endorsements can be sent out with direct mail pieces, a press release, your press kit, or posted on your web site. You could also turn it into a brochure.

5. You can benefit by providing testimonials for others.

At times, it really is "more blessed to give than to receive." As you begin working to collect endorsements from others, don't hesitate to return the favor. In fact, it would help to be deliberate. Instead of waiting to be asked for your testimonial; take the initiative. Send them out whenever you are pleased with a particularly product or service. Doing this will increase your own visibility.

6. You can write it up for your clients or customers.

When I asked a noted author to write a Foreword for one of my books, he said he would be happy to do so.

"Just write up something and I'll take a look at it and sign it," he said.

So I wrote a draft of the Foreword and mailed it to him for his review. He added a couple of sentences and gave me the go-ahead to publish it.

Since then, I have found this to be quite common. So if your satisfied client would like to endorse your work but feels that he or she cannot write it, you can offer to write it for them.

7. Your list of testimonials should remain current.

From time to time, it is useful to change or replace your testimonials. Fresh names suggest ongoing success. So keep an updated list.

Continue to look for testimonials that have strong sales copy and other compelling features. Use these on the front page of your communications. If you're using a full page of testimonials, put your best ones at the top. Picture this scenario:

Let's say you have a list posted on your web site. The endorsements are all good and convincing. But then you learn that the president of a national organization has said some great things about you and your work. Because this president is widely known and well-respected, you rush to get permission to use the comments. The permission is granted.

So you hasten to place that endorsement on the front page of your web site—and at the top of your list of testimonials. This type of experience would be a dream come true. Yet, it illustrates how you can keep your list fresh and vibrant throughout your campaign.

This sums up what you need to know about testimonials. Just remember to be alert to positive feedback and make it your mission to give, as well as receive, kind words about quality products and services.

"Testimonials and letters of recommendation are very valuable to your career," say Dottie and Lilly Walters in *Speak and Grow Rich*. "Some will come to you unsolicited, but most require time, effort, and planning on your part. They are well worth it."

From time to time, it is useful to change or replace your testimonials. Fresh names suggest ongoing success. So keep an updated list.

Chapter 16

15 Tips for Launching an Effective Publicity Campaign
An Action Plan and Blueprint for Your Success

*A*RE YOU READY TO GET STARTED? *W*OULD YOU LIKE TO TAKE WHAT you've learned thus far and put it all into action? If so, then it's time to develop a sensible, and practical plan—one that's flexible, yet firm enough to keep you on target. As you begin to implement the suggestions given throughout this book, remember that the most important thing you need to generate media coverage is *news*. Be on the lookout for fresh news angles and ideas that may emerge during your campaign and be quick to alert the press. If cost is a factor, plan on using about 10 percent of your budget for a 12-month campaign.

This section is basically an action plan that offers a few essential steps for getting your campaign off the ground. Use it as a guide, but nothing more. This way, if you feel the need to change something or maybe do something in a different way, you have that liberty.

1. Develop your unique sales message.

Your unique sales message is the slogan or tag line that sets you apart from all the competition. It should summarize what you do that no one else does.

It should mention a service—or a certain aspect of a service—that no one else has mentioned. To be effective, it must be easy to pronounce and easy to remember. Spend extra time in developing a message that sums up what your company does in a clever, but effective way.

2. Define your objectives

What do you want to accomplish? Do you want to generate more leads? Boost the sale of your products or service? Recruit sales professionals? Or do you want to raise funds for a nonprofit organization? Or raise awareness of a certain issue in order to pressure government leaders?

3. Develop or rent reliable mailing lists

The lists should include media contacts, current customers/clients, and prospects. Make an update as soon as you learn of a change.

4. Collect the media guidelines for submission.

Various newspapers and trade magazines have specific guidelines for submitting work for publication. Request their guidelines or download them from the web. This information will be useful when it's time to publish articles.

Write a few how-to articles that you can send out throughout the year. Ideally, having one published each month would be great for your campaign.

5. Prepare all media documents in advance.

Develop your press kit with the necessary documents: press release, cover letter, bio sheet, fact sheet, photos, brochures, etc. Assuming your campaign will consist of public talks, prepare a few speeches that you can deliver in a moment's notice. Design your talks for specific audiences such as college students, business groups, and social clubs.

Write a few how-to articles that you can send out throughout the year. Ideally, having one published each month would be great for your campaign.

Make sure your web site is up and running. Ensure that it has your unique sales message, relevant products and services, and full contact information. Check it for errors and typos, and to make sure it is reader-friendly and can be easily followed. Leave nothing to chance.

6. Plan a special event for each month of your campaign.

Develop these events as news events, for which you can submit press releases and be covered. The first event should open with a bang. It could be a grand opening, ground breaking, major announcement, publication of a book, or a visit by a celebrity or a top government leader. Whichever approach you choose, be prepared to alert the press.

7. Use the media and direct mail to alert your audience.

When the media publishes your press releases, chances are that many in your audience will see the write-ups. Assuming they do, when they receive your direct mail they will not be in the dark on what you're doing. In fact, they will be more inclined to believe you because of the credibility you have by being published.

Your published newspaper articles can be cut out and inserted as clips and/or fliers inside your direct mail package. This too will enhance your credibility.

8. Become the talker of the town.

Seek out speaking engagements for local social clubs and business groups. If appropriate, contact churches and local schools. Of course, some engagements such as conferences and workshops, require extra lead time and must be planned far in advance. Because of this, they might not fit in your current campaign. Yet, you can always use them for future campaigns. Remember: Always notify the press of your engagements.

9. Use public meetings as networking opportunities.

Make it a practice to collect business cards and ask for referrals and recommendations. Where practical, hand out your cards, as well.

10. Unleash your articles to trade journals and e-zines.

Tip sheets and how-to articles are some of the easiest to publish. Begin sending out queries each month to magazines in your field. Offer shorter articles, 200 to 300 words, to online newsletters. Typically, these articles are offered freely but they should include your Resource Box which will direct readers to your web site.

As soon as one article is published, submit another to that publication. Keep it up and you may be invited to write a column.

11. Pyramid your published work.

Use your press clips as brochures or fliers. Hand them out to customers. Send them to clients and prospects. Include them in your press kit. When you're featured in a magazine, write a press release about the feature and send it to your local newspaper.

Let your web site reflect this coverage. Example: "Featured in _____!" You may also have this announced at your speaking engagements.

12. Piggyback on current events.

Become a news junkie and look for ways you can tie in your promotion to the big story. When you recognize a particular angle, fire off a press release to the media.

13. Become a news analyst for the media.

Make yourself available to the media as an expert in your field. Present your credentials and any demo tapes or recordings of you in action. Do your homework and be ready for tough questions. You may wait for reporters to call you, or you can take the initiative and contact them when news breaks.

14. Be prepared for the unexpected.

Unfortunately, bad things do happen. And they often happen at the worst of times. While you could not possibly anticipate accidents, you can prepare for them by setting into place a plan of action. For instance, if you become ill and cannot speak or give interviews, designate a substitute. If something is reported that portrays your business in a negative light, be quick to respond. Don't wait.

15. Check your progress.

Be ready to change or revise any feature that is not working. Keep a close eye on the media and keep track of your clips. Test all of your direct mail response and don't forget the traffic to your web site. The knowledge you gain by analyzing your progress will make you better equipped for your next campaign.

As we bring this section to a close, I think an old proverb is worth repeating: "If you fail to plan, you plan to fail." It's trite but true. Take time today to begin working on a plan for promoting your products or services. Write down all the required steps and make a list of the documents you need. Discuss this with a staff member, manager, or friend. Once everything is in place, drive full-speed ahead.

If you fail to plan, you plan to fail. It's trite but true. Take time today to begin working on a plan for promoting your products or services.

Appendixes

Appendix A

Bibliography/
Recommended Reading

Adair-Hoy, Angela. *Profitable Email Publishing*. Bangor, ME: Deep South Publishing Co./Booklocker.com, 2001.

Anthony, Dr. Robert. *How to Make a Fortune from Public Speaking*. New York: Berkley Books, 1983.

Adams, Charles F. *Common Sense in Advertising*. New York: McGraw-Hill, 1965.

Antin, H. Brad and Alan J. Antin. *Secrets from the Lost Art of Common Sense Marketing*. Clearwater, FL: The Antin Marketing Group, 1992.

Benson, Richard V. *Secrets of Successful Direct Mail*. Lincolnwood, IL: NTC Business Books, 1989.

Barnes III, Roscoe. *Big Bucks from Little Sketches*. Gettysburg, PA: McKinley & Henson, 1993.

_____. *The Better Letter*. Philadelphia, PA: Target Marketing Group/NAPCO, 2006

_____. *Direct Response Marketing Made Easy*. California: Entrepreneur Press, 2007.

_____. *Discover Your Talent and Find Fulfillment*. Gettysburg, PA: McKinley & Henson, 1992.

_____. *Scooping the Competition*. Waynesboro, PA: Roscoe Barnes III, 1998.

_____. *Secrets of a Writing Hustler*. Kandiyohi, MN: Filbert Publishing, 2004.

_____. *The Guide to Effective Gospel Tract Ministry*. Elkton, MD: Church Growth Institute, 2004.

Bayan, Richard. *Words that Sell*. Lincolnwood, IL: Contemporary Books, 1984.

Bly, Robert W. *Ads that Sell*. Brentwood, New York: Asher-Gallant Press, 1988.

_____. *The Copywriter's Handbook*. New York: Owl Books, 2005.

_____. *Targeted Public Relations*. New York: Henry Holt & Co., 1993.

Blake, Gary and Robert W. Bly. *The Elements of Copywriting*. New York: Macmillan, 1997.

Blanco, Jodee. *The Complete Guide to Book Publicity*. New York: Allworth Press, 2000.

Bodian, Nat G. *Direct Marketing Rules of Thumb*. New York: McGraw-Hill, Inc., 1995.

_____. *How to Choose a Winning Title*. Phoenix, AZ: The Oryx Press, 1989.

Benson, Richard V. *Secrets of Successful Direct Mail*. Lincolnwood, IL: NTC Business Books, 1989.

Bivins, Thomas. *Handbook for Public Relations*. Lincolnwood, IL: NTC Business Books, 1989.

Bovee, Cortland L. and William F. Arens. *Contemporary Advertising*. Homewood, IL: Richard D. Irwin Inc., 1982.

Bowerman, Peter. *The Well-Fed Writer*. Atlanta, GA: Fanove Publishing, 2000.

Caples, John. *How to Make Your Advertising Make Money*. Englewood Cliffs, NJ: Prentice-Hall, 1983.

_____. *Tested Advertising Methods*. Englewood Cliffs, NJ: Prentice-Hall, 1974.

Digregorio, Charlotte. *Beginner's Guide to Writing and Selling Quality Features*. Portland, OR: Civetta Press, 1990.

Ferdi, Liz. *Successful Direct Mail*. Hauppauge, NY: Barron's Educational Series Inc., 1997.

Garrison, Bruce. *Professional News Writing*. Hillsdale, NJ: Lawrence Erlbaum Associates Publishers, 1990.

Gauss, Chester A. and Lucius I. Wightman. *Practical Business Administration, Vol. III, Advertising*. Chicago: American Technical Society, 1935.

Glim, Aesop. *Copy—The Core of Advertising*. New York: McGraw-Hill, 1949.

Gosden Jr., Freeman F. *Direct Marketing Success*. New York: John Wiley & Sons, 1985.

Hahn, Fred E. *Do-It-Yourself Advertising*. New York: John Wiley & Sons Inc., 1993.

Hicks, Tyler G. *Mail Order Success Secrets*. Rocklin, CA: Prima Publishing, 1992.

Hoelscher, Russ von. *How You Can Make a Fortune Selling Information by Mail*. San Diego: Profit Ideas, 1988.

Hopkins, Claude C. *My Life in Advertising & Scientific Advertising*. Lincolnwood, IL: NTC Business Books, 1995.

Howard, Lee. *$50,000 a Year from Mail Order Ads*. Forth Worth, TX: Premier Publishers, 1988.

_____. *Mail Order Success Secrets*. Clearwater, FL: Selective Books Inc., 1994.

Kalian, Robert. *Mail Order Success Secrets*. White Plains, NY: Roblin Press, 1998.

Kennedy, Daniel S. *The Ultimate Marketing Plan*. Holbrook, MA: Adams Media Corp., 2000.

_____. *The Ultimate Sales Letter*. Holbrook, MA: Bob Adams Inc., 1990.

Kleppner, Otto, Russell Thomas, and Glenn Verrill. *Otto Kleppner's Advertising Procedure*, 8th Edition. Englewood Cliffs, NJ: Prentice-Hall Inc., 1983.

Lant, Jeffrey, Ph.D. *Cash Copy*. Cambridge: JLA Publications, 1989.

_____. *No More Cold Calls*. Cambridge: JLA Publications, 1993.

_____. *The Unabashed Self-Promoter's Guide*. JLA Publications, 1983.

Levinson, Jay Conrad. *Guerrilla Advertising*. Boston: Houghton Mifflin Co., 1994.

_____. *Guerrilla Marketing*. Boston: Houghton Mifflin Co., 1993.

_____, Rick Frishman and Jill Lublin. *Guerrilla Publicity*. Avon, MA: Adams Media Corp., 2002.

Lewis, Gordon Herschell. *Direct Mail Copy that Sells*. Englewood Cliffs, NJ: Prentice Hall Inc., 1984.

_____. *On the Art of Writing Copy*, 3rd Edition. Racom Communications, 2003.

_____. *Sales Letters that Sizzle*, 2nd Edition. Chicago, IL: NTC Business Books, 1999.

Margolis, Charles. *How to Write Copy that Sells*. Cleveland, OH: Speedibooks, 1987.

Nicholas, Ted. *Publish and Promote Your Own Book*. Canada: Coles Publishing Company Ltd., 1981.

_____. *Magic Words that Bring You Riches*. Indian Rocks Beach, FL: Nicholas Direct Inc., 1995.

Ogilvy, David. *Confessions of an Advertising Man*. New York: Macmillan, 1987.

_____. *Ogilvy on Advertising*. New York: Vintage, 1985.

Perrin, Carl. *So You Want to Be a Writer*. Auburn, CA: eBookstand Books, 2002.

Powers, Melvin. *How to Get Rich in Mail Order*. No. Hollywood, CA: Wilshire Book Company, 1998.

Provost, Gary. *100 Ways to Improve Your Writing*. New York: New American Library, 1985.

Rohrer, Norman B. *Discover Your Possibilities in Writing*. Hume Lake, CA: Christian Writers Guild, 1992.

Roman, Kenneth and Jane Maas. *How to Advertise*, 2nd Edition. New York: St. Martin's Griffin, 1992.

Rose, M.J. and Angela Adair-Hoy. *How to Publish and Promote Online*. New York: St. Martin's Griffen, 2001.

Reecher, David A. and Jerry Buchanan. *Maxwell Sackheim's Billion Dollar Marketing Concepts and Applications*. Vancouver, WA: TOWERS Club USA Press, 1966.

Safire, William and Leonard Sifir. *Good Advice on Writing*. New York, Simon & Schuster, 1992.

Sackheim, Maxwell. *How to Advertise Yourself*. New York: Macmillan, 1978.

Schwab, Victor. *How to Write a Good Advertisement*. Hollywood, CA: Wilshire, 1962.

Schwartz, Eugene M. *Breakthrough Advertising*. New York: Boardroom Books, 1984.

Scott, Dewitt H. *Secrets of Successful Writing*. Harrisonburg, VA: Christian Light Publications, 1998.

Strunk Jr., William and E.B. White. *The Elements of Style*, 4th Edition. New York. Longman, 2000.

Stilson, Galen. *59 Response/Profit Tips, Tricks & Techniques*. Fort Worth, TX: Premier Publishers Inc., 1997.

_____. *How to Make the Successful Transition from Small-Time to Big-Time Mail Order ... on a Limited Budget*. Fort Worth, TX: Premier Publishers Inc., 1996.

_____. *How to Write and Design Money-Making Response Advertisements*. Fort Worth, TX: Premier Publishers Inc., 1997.

_____. *How You Can Write Winning Sales Letters*. Fort Worth, TX: Premier Publishers Inc., 1998.

_____. *The Success How-to's of Money-Making Direct Mail*. Fort Worth, TX: Premier Publishers Inc., 1998.

Sugarman, Joseph. *Marketing Secrets of a Mail Order Maverick*. Las Vegas, NV: DelStar Books, 1998.

Tighe, John Francis. *Making Money with Mail*. Wellfleet, MA: PMT Press, 1993.

Vitale, Joe. *Cyber Writing*. New York: AMACOM, 1997.

_____. *The AMA Complete Guide to Small Business Advertising*. Lincolnwood, IL: NTC Business Books, 1995.

_____. *There's a Customer Born Every Minute*. New York: AMACOM, 1998.

_____. *The Seven Lost Secrets of Success*. Awareness Publications.

Zinsser, William. *On Writing Well*, 5th Edition. New York: HaperCollins Publishers, 1994.

Walters, Dottie and Lilly Walters. *Speak and Grow Rich*. Paramus, NJ: Prentice-Hall, 1997.

Watkins, Julian Lewis. *The 100 Greatest Advertisements*. Toronto, Canada: Coles Publishing Co. Ltd., 1959.

Williamson, Daniel R. *Feature Writing for Newspapers*. New York: Hastings House Publishers, 1975.

Appendix B

Sample Press Release

FOR IMMEDIATE RELEASE

Roscoe Barnes III
P.O. Box 803
Waynesboro, Pa. 17268
Phone: 717-762-6806
E-mail: Roscoe@roscoebarnes.net

NEW BOOK SHOWS REPORTERS HOW TO BEAT THEIR COMPETITION

WAYNESBORO, Pa.—A Pennsylvania reporter believes the antidote for boredom, low pay, and other problems in the newsroom, can be found in one word: Scoop.

"There's nothing like a good scoop," says Roscoe Barnes III. "It can transform a newsroom, boost morale, increase readership, and excite reporters, while bringing them respect and other rewards."

Barnes, a reporter for the Waynesboro (Pa.) Record Herald, is the author of Scooping the Competition: How to Be First in Reporting Hot Stories. Based on his 18 years of experience as an award-winning journalist, the book shows reporters—beginners and veterans—how to hone their skills for maximum results.

It gives proven techniques for breaking stories of great significance. Among other things, readers are shown:

- ▶ How to recognize a hot story
- ▶ How to find good tipsters
- ▶ How to dress for success
- ▶ How to win friends and influence sources
- ▶ How to study, beat, and get even with the competition
- ▶ How to "crash" a press conference
- ▶ What to do when an editor says "No." And much more.

"Good reporting is a proactive and competitive endeavor that relies on creativity and determination," says Barnes. "To excel, one must have the instincts of a scholar, the eyes of a detective, the ears of a counselor, and the guts of a warrior."

With that in mind, Barnes uses research and personal anecdotes to show:

- ▶ Why people skills can sometimes be more valuable than documents when gathering news.
- ▶ What every reporter can learn from a preacher, counselor, military general, and marketer.
- ▶ What print reporters can learn from their TV competitors.
- ▶ How becoming an author can help in generating tips for good stories.

Scooping the Competition is published by the author as an oversized study guide (8½ × 11, comb-bound, 130 pages). It sells for $39.95. To order, write to: Roscoe Barnes III, P.O. Box 803, Waynesboro, Pa. 17268.

A free sample excerpt entitled, "8 Great Benefits of Beating the Competition," is available for the asking. Editors and reporters may request it by mail or by calling the author at 717-762-6806. Barnes may also be reached at roscoe@roscoebarnes.net.

—End—

Press Release News Topics

Any of the items featured in this list would be suitable for a press release. All of the topics are newsworthy and will generate interest by newspapers and/or magazines because they either contain news, entertainment, a human interest element, or useful information.

Opening of new business
Celebrity endorsements
Political endorsements
Expert endorsements
Ground-breaking ceremony
Job promotion
Purchase of new business
School graduation
Book signings and readings
Special donation
Charity fundraiser
Special meetings with celebrities or government leaders
Sponsorship of nonprofit events
Awards and certification
Major purchases (of property or products)
Recognition of employees
Open House
Business or plant tours
Publication of books and articles
Launching of newsletter
Workshops and seminars
Contests or sweepstakes
Lectures
Business breakfast/lunch
Business conference
Special achievements
Unusual promotions
Special trips
Unusual products and services
New product
Old product with new name
Expert opinion on any subject

New employees
Research
Survey or poll results
Major contracts award to your company
Comment on breaking news
Tips and how-to advice
Disagreement with major news story
Special events
Press conference
Business emergences
Disasters
New partnerships
Joint ventures
Company reorganizations
New company logo and/or slogan

Appendix C

Sample Queries

Query for Book Idea

To: Filbert Publishing

Dear Mrs. Beth Erickson:

As a 12-year-old black kid in the Mississippi Delta, I chopped cotton, raised hogs and plowed fields to help support my family of 11. Today, at 42, I'm an award-winning journalist, and former columnist for two national publications. I'm also a full-time copywriter whose words are used each day to sell millions of dollars worth of products and services.

Despite the odds—and the mounds of rejection slips—that were stacked against me, I wrote my way to the top. And I did it using a number of proven, creative strategies that guarantee success. Those winning strategies are all revealed in:

Secrets of a Writing Hustler: How to Beat the Odds, Overcome Rejection—and Succeed as a Writer

Although scores of books have been written on various aspects of writing, most are either too narrow or too broad in their focus to benefit the struggling writer.

Secrets of a Writing Hustler is a "*Confessions of an Advertising Man* meets *On Writing Well*." As such, it is part memoir and part how-to. The 200-page guide is a "one-stop shop" for freelance writers, journalists, copywriters, and entrepreneurs. Most of the chapters first appeared in the columns I wrote for *Fund Raising Management magazine* and *Publishers' Auxiliary*.

The advice in *Secrets of a Writing Hustler* is based on my 20-plus years of experience as a journalist, copywriter, author, and freelance writer for magazines. To date, I've authored seven books and training guides (some self-published). And I've had gospel tracts published by some of the leading Christian publishing houses.

Is this a topic that would be suitable for your publishing house? I have included an outline of the proposed book. And I would be happy to send you a detailed proposal and/or the completed manuscript.

What do you think?

Roscoe Barnes III

Query for Column Idea

To: Writer's Journal

Dear Mr. Leon Ogroske:

I almost cried the first time I was paid for a copywriting assignment.

I'd spent only three hours writing a two-page sales letter. I sent it to my client and waited, almost biting my nails with fear and anxiety. Two days later, the client sent me a note that showered me with praise and she included a check for $2,000.

Imagine that! A nice $2,000 for only three hours of work! Fortunately, my experience is not uncommon. In fact, it can be easily duplicated by other writers.

For this reason, I'd like to propose a column on copywriting for the *Writers' Journal*. It would offer tips on good writing techniques, pointers for creating all types of commercial copy, lessons in marketing and self-promotion, and advice on how to get high-paying assignments.

By way of introduction, I should mention that I am an award-winning journalist (with over 20 years experience), author of numerous books (some self-published) and seminar leader. My articles have appeared in many trade publications, including the *Writers' Journal* ("How to Write Features with Impact"), *Editor & Publisher, Writer's Forum, Authorship, Enrichment Journal, Grace in Focus*, and plenty of others.

I used to write the column, "Copy Thoughts," for *Fund Raising Management* magazine (Hoke Communications Inc.); and "Streetwise Reporting," for Publishers' Auxiliary (National Newspaper Association). I've been a selling copywriter for over 15 years.

Unlike freelancing for magazines and newspapers, copywriting is one of the most lucrative forms of writing. You don't always get a byline, but you quickly earn money to pay bills and keep food on the table.

Would you be interested in such a column?

If so, I would gladly provide you with more details on my background, including samples of my work. Let me know what you think.

Roscoe Barnes III

Query for Column Idea

(Sent as e-mail)

To: Tidal Wave Business Newsmagazine

From: "Roscoe Barnes" <Roscoe@roscoebarnes.net >

To: <editor@kineticwavellc.com>

Sent: Thursday, June 15, 2006 8:32 AM

Subject: Question about writing a column

Dear Ms. Gail Williams:

Is your paper, *The Tidal Wave Newspaper*, open to a new column on Marketing and Advertising?

If so, I'd like to submit a proposal and samples of my work for your consideration.

Thanks.

Roscoe

Roscoe Barnes III
Author, Copywriter, Ghostwriter
Bio: www.writers.net/writers/31854
Phone: (717) 762-6806
E-mail: Roscoebarnes3@yahoo.com

Query Follow-Up

Dear Ms. Williams:

Many thanks for your reply and your interest in my proposed column idea. Below is an outline of what I have in mind. Samples of my work have been submitted in separate emails.

If approved, the column may be published free of charge in exchange for a generous bio section or free ad space.

I'm still undecided on what to call the column. So far I've selected the following:

- ▶ Kinetic Marketing Ideas
- ▶ Another Marketing Moment
- ▶ Your Marketing Response
- ▶ Steady Marketing
- ▶ On Marketing Ripples
- ▶ Your Marketing Waves

I considered titles such as "Marketing Tips," "Marketing Ideas" and "Easy Marketing," but a quick search with Google showed they were all taken. Too bad.

At any rate, I'm open to your suggestion.

Let me know if you have questions or need more information. If you prefer a phone call, I can call anytime before 11 a.m. or after 8 p.m.

Regards

Roscoe

Proposal

Steady Marketing: Ideas and Tips to Help You Sell More of Your Products and Services

"This is the one source for practical, creative and streetwise tips for maximized marketing, publicity and advertising!"

Introduction

Steady Marketing by Roscoe Barnes III would be a monthly column for entrepreneurs and small business professionals that shows them how to push their marketing efforts to the next level. It will provide tips, techniques, strategies, and advice for selling more of their products and services.

The column can be written at any length requested by the editor, but without such request, it will average between 500 and 900 words. The editor may edit or cut for length or style without the author's permission.

Based on my 20-plus years of experience as an award-winning journalist, and more than 10 years as a copywriter, author, and marketing consultant, the column will be intensely practical and easy to follow.

It will show how any businessperson can use proven techniques to boost profits, increase store traffic, generate hot leads, and increase visibility, among other things.

Contents

Readers will be given a full measure of examples, colorful anecdotes, book reviews, comments from the experts, lessons from life, humor, history and tidbits of commentary.

What readers can expect:

- ► Loads of useful information and practical, hands-on advice taken from real life experience. In short, it will be light on theory and heavy on practical techniques that get results.

- ► Proven strategies and tactics for: generating leaders; catching customers or clients through direct mail (and email); and launching effective marketing or publicity campaigns, among other topics.

- ► Sound advice that is both instructional and motivational. It will be straight-forward and yet, inspirational. It will draw on case studies and history as they relate to the topic.

- ► Informative reviews of books and other tools and resources that are useful to the ambitious business professional.

- ► Insightful quotes from businesspeople throughout the Washington-Baltimore areas.

▶ Answers and opinions on tough marketing questions, as well as Q&A–type interviews that can serve as "Profiles" or "Success Stories" of area experts and businesspeople.

Sample Topics

Since the column will primarily be how-to in nature, it will cover the gamut of marketing ideas. It will include such topics as:

▶ How to write attention-getting ads, brochures, and sales letters

▶ How to design powerful direct mail packages

▶ How to write the ultimate press release

▶ How to deal with the media

▶ How to become recognized as an expert in your field

▶ How to stump the competition

▶ How to woo clients and close deals

▶ How to craft feature stories that generate business…and lots more!

Note: The column's subject matter can be tailored to special themes suggested by the editor.

Rights Offered

One-time rights are offered for print media only. Rights for online, electronic, or other forms of publication may be available through negotiation.

Each column will appear with the following copyright information: "Copyright © Date:____ by Roscoe Barnes III."

Delivery

The column may be delivered as hard copy by regular mail or by email (as text inside email or as Word file attachment).

Author's Information

It is requested that in lieu of payment, each column will include a photo of the author and a generous "Resource Box" or "Author's Bio" section.

An example of the "Resource Box" would be as follows:

"Roscoe Barnes III is an award-winning journalist, copywriter, ghostwriter and marketing consultant. He's the author of numerous books, including *Secrets of a Writing Hustler* (Filbert Publishing, 2005), *Direct Response Advertising Made Easy* (Entrepreneur Press, 2007), *The Better Letter* (Target Marketing Group, 2006), and *The Guide to Effective Gospel Tract Ministry* (Church Growth Institute, 2004). Barnes can be reached at (717)-762-6806 or Roscoe@roscoebarnes.net. For more information, visit: www.roscoebarnes.net.

Query for News Coverage

To: The Gettysburg Times

Dear Editor:

Ever hear of an "Environmental Christmas"?

That's what we're having. And we're using this chance to offer free help to people needing boxes to wrap their gifts.

How is this done? Recycling.

We're taking "throw-aways" from area businesses and recycling them into clean boxes and package stuffings to help people with their mailings.

May we ask you to do a feature on this? To our knowledge, we're the first and only business in town to do something of this nature.

If this interests you, please call me any time. I'd be happy to discuss it further.

Many thanks for your time and consideration.

Sincerely,

(Business owner)

P.S. We're now under new management and offer new services. Hope to hear from you.

Appendix D

Sample Feature Article

SELF-ESTEEM GROWS AS THE POUNDS DROP

90-Pound Weight Loss Changes Local Woman's Life
by Roscoe Barnes III

Martha Blattenberger gets stares and lots of compliments everywhere she goes. Friends who haven't seen her in a while often walk up and lean toward her with a curious squint.

"Do I know you?" they ask. "You look like somebody I used to know."

"Of course, you know me," Blattenberger tells them. "I used to be a lot heavier."

Blattenberger, 27, once weighed 225 pounds. Today she tips the scale at 135. Because of her dramatic 90-pound weight loss—which took place in only nine months—she is featured in a television commercial for LA Weight Loss Center. It began airing this week on Channel 8.

Blattenberger, who once ran from cameras, shunned crowds and sometimes hid in her home, is now a different person. At 5-feet, 8-inches, she walks today with the sleek, trim figure of a fashion queen. Her back is erect and her features glamorous.

"My husband, Paul, says I'm a new woman now," she says with a grin. "I feel like a new person. I can't stay at home. I want to go out and be around other people. I feel good about myself."

Blattenberger is the mother of two children: Taylor, 4 and Margo, 14 months. She and her family live in Zullinger.

On a sunny Wednesday afternoon, Blattenberger sat down to talk about her new self.

"My 10-year class reunion is next year," she begins, flashing a cover-girl smile. "I'm looking forward to it."

As a student at Waynesboro Area Senior High School, Blattenberger weighed 160 pounds. After school, she got married, had children and put on the pounds. And for four years, she says, she was "very overweight."

When It All Started

Blattenberger started gaining weight while pregnant with her son Taylor. She encountered a problem known as toxemia that caused her to put on a lot of water weight. In fact, she eventually weighed 10 pounds more than her husband.

"He told me that he loves me no matter what," she recalls.

Still, she thought the worst.

"I could imagine people seeing us walking down the streets and asking, 'What's he doing with this big fat thing?'"

In anticipation of actually losing the weight, Blattenberger purchased 12 pairs of size 14 jeans and slacks, believing one day she would wear them again. After Margo was born, her husband asked her about her promise.

He didn't harass her or give her a hard time, she says. He merely asked a question. And that's the way she took it, although an answer didn't come easily.

But one day while watching her children play, she found a good incentive. "I didn't want to be a fat mom," Blattenberger says. "I wanted to be able to run and play with my children. I also wanted to be healthy overall."

Another day, she was visiting with her parents, Marvin Ray and Martha Kirby, and picked up *The Record Herald*, where she saw an LA Weight Loss Center ad.

She called the center and arranged for her first visit.

"I had tried Slim Fast, little diets in magazines, but nothing worked," she says. She would lose pounds and gain them back. "I felt like I was going down a dead-end street."

This time it would be different. At the center, she found one-on-one personal counseling and no starvation diet plans. For the most part, she followed a diet that was high in protein and low in carbohydrates. She also drank more than 64 ounces of water each day.

First Three Days

First was a three-day preparation phase, where she ate two eggs a day, green salad with fat-free salad dressing, an unlimited amount of red meat, a teaspoon of lite salt, two oranges and water.

During that brief time, she lost 7 pounds—and was never hungry.

As her program progressed, she pulled out her stationary bike at home "which had collected dust." She began using it 10 to 20 minutes twice a week. Then she increased to four to six times a week at 30 to 40 minutes a shot.

What began as a dreaded task became a treasured habit, she says. Her husband, who has always been the athletic type, offered a little coaching here and there, she says, but she was mostly on her own.

"I did crunches and calf raises," she says. "Sometimes I would get really mad with Paul and tell him to leave me alone."

Month after month, the pounds vanished until Blattenberger became lighter than she was in high school. Her initial goal was to weigh 150 pounds, but she surpassed that. And before long, she retrieved the sized 14 pants she'd saved for four years. They were now too big, as she is a size 6.

"She definitely is a new woman," Paul says. "Her looks and her attitude have changed. She has a better outlook on life."

Husband Amazed

Paul says he is amazed and keeps telling her how great she looks.

"As her husband, I think she's the most beautiful woman there is," he says. "But losing the weight makes her feel a lot more confident. I'm proud of her."

Both of them agree that she lost the weight for herself and no one else.

On July 4, the couple took a trip to Ocean City along with Martha's mother.

"I've always loved the beach," Martha says. "When I was heavy, I hated to go out in a bathing suit."

This time she did it with pleasure.

As she strutted across the sands, men everywhere began to gawk and smile.

Martha's mother and her husband noticed it and remarked, "Those men are checking you out."

"That's fine," Martha said. "Let 'em look."

Appendix E

Recommended Periodicals

Advertising Age
711 Third Ave.
New York, NY 10017
Phone: 212-210-0100
www.adage.com

Adweek
70 Broadway
New York, NY 10003
Phone: 646-654-5421
www.adweek.com

B-to-B
360 N. Michigan Ave.
Chicago, IL 60601
www.btobonline.com

Direct
http://directmag.com

Direct Marketing
224 Seventh St.
Garden City, NY 11530
Phone: 516-746-6700
www.dmcny.org

DM News
100 Avenue of the Americas
New York, NY 10013
Phone: 212-925-7300
www.dmnews.com

Entrepreneur Magazine
Phone: 800-274-6229
www.entrepreneur.com

FundRaising Success
1500 Spring Garden St., Suite 1200
Philadelphia, PA 19130
Phone: 215-238-5300

Home Business Magazine
Phone: 714-968-0331
www.homebusinessmag.com

Inside Direct Mail
1500 Spring Garden St., Suite 1200
Philadelphia, PA 19130-4094

Money Making Opportunities
Success Publishing International
11071 Ventura Blvd.
Studio City, CA 91604
Phone: 818-980-9166

Public Relations Journal
33 Maiden Lane, 11th Flr.
New York, NY 10038
Phone: 212-460-1400
www.prsa.org

Publishers' Auxiliary
Stan Schwartz, Editor
(573) 882-6327
tan@nna.org
P.O. Box 7540
Columbia, MO 65205-7540

Sales and Marketing Management
770 Broadway 7th Flr.
New York, NY 10003
Phone: 800-641-2030
www.salesandmarketing.com

Target Marketing
1500 Spring Garden St., Suite 1200
Philadelphia, PA 19130
Phone: 215-238-5300
www.targetonline.com

The Tidal Wave Business News Magazine
9400 Snowden River Pkwy.
Suite #110 - PMB#281
Columbia, MD 21045
Phone: 877-660-3175
www.kineticwavellc.com

Writers Journal
P.O. Box 394
Perham, MN 56573
Phone: 218-346-7921
www.writersjournal.com

Appendix F

Recommended Online Newsletters

THERE ARE MANY ONLINE MAGAZINES/NEWSLETTERS/E-ZINES THAT provide practical, easy-to-use tips on various aspects of marketing, writing, and advertising. Those listed below are just a few of the many that should prove helpful in crafting effective direct response advertising copy.

Audacious Marketing Mastery by Deborah McLaughlin & Juanita Bellavance
www.audaciousmarketingmastery.com

Bencivenga's Bullets
www.bencivengabullets.com

The Book Coach Says by Judy Cullins
www.bookcoaching.com

Booklet Tips by Paulette
www.tipsbooklets.com

B-to-B Marketing Online
www.btobonline.com

C.J. Hayden's Get Clients Now
info@getclientsnow.com

Contact Any Celebrity by Jordan McAuley
www.ContactAnyCelebrity.com

Debbie Allen's Shameless Self-Promotion Newsletter
Debbie@DebbieAllen.com

The Direct Response Letter
www.bly.com

The E-zine Queen's Publish for Profits
www.ezinequeen.com

Excess Voice
www.nickusborne.com/excess-voice.htm

Early to Rise
www.earlytorise.com

The Golden Thread Online
www.awaionline.com/thegoldenthread/index.php

The Health Care Marketing Connection Newsletter by Kelly Robbins
www.kellyrobbinsllc.com

Ivan Levison's Levison Letter
ivan@levison.com

Joe Sabah's Stroke of Genius
joe@joesabah.com or Jsabah@aol.com

Joe Robson's Copywriter's Digest
www.adcopywriting.com/Newsletter_Subsc.htm

John Forde's Copywriters' Roundtable
www.jackforde.com

Ken Blum's Black Ink Newsletter
Blummer@aol.com

Marketing Minute
www.yudkin.com/markmin.htm

The MarketSmart Newsletter
www.bookmarketingprofits.com/page4.html

Mequoda Daily by Don Nicholas
mequodadaily@e.mailzeen.com

Money the Write Way
www.moneythewriteway.com

News You Can Use by Joe Vitale
www.mrfire.com

Dr Nunley's Marketing Newsletter
http://drnunley.com/newsletter.htm

Pam Lontos's Newsletter
pam@prpr.net

Paul Hartunian's Million-Dollar Publicity Strategies
www.prprofits.com

Peter "The Humorator" Fogel's Humor This! Ezine: Mining Currets Events for Humor
peter@fortune500comedy.com

Publishing Poynters by Dan Poynter
www.parapublishing.com

Quick Tips from Marketing Mentor by Ilise Benun
http://www.marketing-mentor.com/html/tips.html

Dr. Ralph Wilson's Web Marketing Today
www.wilsonweb.com

Raleigh Pinskey's Newsletter
Raleigh@PromoteYourself.com

The Success Margin
www.tednicholas.com

Susan Harrow's 60 Second Secrets Newsletter
60secondsecrets@prsecrets.com

Target Marketing Tipline
www.targetmarketingmag.com

Tips & Updates from Writer's Digest
www.writersdigest.com

The Total Package by Clayton Makepeace
www.makepeacetotalpackage.com

The Well-Fed Writer by Peter Bowerman
www.wellfedwriter.com

The Web Marketing Advisor by Daniel Levis
www.web-marketingadvisor.com

Writing Etc.
www.filbertpublishing.com

Writing for Dollars
www.writingfordollars.com

WritersWeekly Newsletter
www.writersweekly.com

Appendix G

Recommended Bloggers and Other Online Resources

Bloggers

This list consists of professional copywriters, authors, and publishers.

Angela Adair-Hoy
www.writersweekly.com

Bob Bly
www.bly.com

Beth Erickson
www.filbertpublishing.com

Clayton Makepeace
www.makepeacetotalpackage.com

Denny Hatch's Business Common Sense
www.targetmarketingmag.com

Dianne Huff's B-2-B Marketing
www.marcom-writer-blog.com/

Ilise Benun
www.marketing-mentor.com

Joe Vitale
www.mrfire.com

John Kremer on Marketing
www.publishersmarketplace.com/members/JohnKremer

Judy Cullins
www.bookcoaching.com

Kelly Robbins
www.kellyrobbinsllc.com

Marcia Yudkin
www.yudkin.com/markmin.htm

M.J. Rose's Buzz, Balls & Hype
www.publishersmarketplace.com/members/BkDoctorSin

Paulette Ensign
www.tipsbooklets.com

Peter Bowerman
www.wellfedwriter.com

Richard Armstrong
richardarmstrong.blogspot.com

Discussion Groups

Although most of these groups focus on the general aspects of writing for publication, some include business professionals who offer tips and advice on copywriting. One in particular (AWAI) has students who post questions about all areas of copywriting.

AbsoluteWrite
www.absolutewrite.com
Provides a forum with advice on types of writing issues, including copywriting and writing for publication.

American Writers and Artists Institute (AWAI)
www.awaionline.com
Provides detailed and enlightening discussion on all aspects of commercial writing.

Angela Adair-Hoy's Group
www.writersweekly.com

Provides forum for discussion on writing and publishing, as well as advice for determining legitimate publishers.

Beth Erickson and Vicky Heron's Group
http://finance.groups.yahoo.com/group/CopywriterMastermind or www.filbertpublishing.com
Provides detailed questions and answers with practical advice for copywriting and self-promotion.

www.writers.net
Provides listing of agents, authors, editors, publishers, and discussion forum for all aspects of writing and publishing.

Web Sites

American Writers and Artists Institute (AWAI)
www.awaionline.com
Provides home-study course, conferences, and helpful discussion forum.

About Public Relations
www.aboutpublicrelations.net/basics.htm
Provides answers to tough questions about public relations.

Bob Bly
www.bly.com
Provides scores of free articles on different types of writing along with useful listings of vendors and other resources.

Cyber Speaker
www.cyberspeaker.com/nsapress.html
Provides tips for generating media interviews and news coverage.

Entrepreneur
www.entrepreneur.com
Provides e-zines, articles, books, and everything you ever wanted to know about starting and running a successful business.

e-Releases
http://www.ereleases.com/pr/prfuel.html
Provides guidelines and ideas for crafting effective press releases.

Joe Vitale
www.mrfire.com
Provides tons of free articles with advice on copywriting and publicity.

Monthly Copywriting Genius
www.monthlycopywritinggenius.com
Provides interviews with copywriters and frequent reviews of successful promotions.

Power Public Relations
http://www.powerpr.com/
Provides many useful resources for promoting businesses and nonprofit enterprises.

Publicity Goldmine
http://www.publicitygoldmine.com/
Provides proven techniques for getting thousands of dollars worth of free publicity.

The Publicity Insider
http://www.publicityinsider.com/pifaq.asp
Provides numerous articles on publicity techniques.

Public Relations Leads
http://www.prleads.com
Provides many practical tips and ideas for generating publicity.

The Small Business Advocate
www.smallbusinessadvocate.com
Provides a radio show and web site with practical information for small businesses.

Spread the News
http://www.spreadthenewspr.com/index.html
Provides essential guidelines for public relations campaigns.

Appendix H

Sample E-zines

Sample E-zine #1
Peter Fogel's "Humor This! E-zine"

To: "Roscoe Barnes" <roscoebarnes3@yahoo.com>
From: "Peter 'The Humorator' Fogel" <peter@fortune500comedy.com>
Date: Mon, 02 Oct 2006 10:27:29 -0500
Subject: Humor This! E-zine: Mining Currents Events for Humor!

Dear Roscoe,

You are receiving this e-mail because you signed up for my Humor This! E-zine. If you can, please inform your spam filters that I am "friend" and not "foe." :)

The purpose of this e-zine is to make you laugh and learn and to show you how to find your "humor eye" that will empower you to overcome the many obstacles you face in life.

Its second purpose is to also present to you power humor techniques that you can use to give more powerful and effective speeches.

Don't forget: when you use humor correctly... if they're laughing...they're listening (to your content).

One of the humor strategies that I preach about is to exploit current events. Humor, as you know, works best when it's unexpected and comes off as being "fresh" to your audience.

Here's an example. Do you remember when there were tire blow outs on the road with Ford's SUVs that used Firestone tires?

The news hit the media like a Tsunami that day. Well, that night on stage while performing I opened my show with a "hang dog" depressed look.

I said, "Well, folks … I hope you're all in a good mood tonight. Two days ago I bought stock in Firestone. (beat; laughter) Who knew?"

I got a great (HUGE) response from the audience. Why? Because it was current and because I committed to the joke fully. And you can easily do the same!

So let's update it. I could not believe that when crazy Venezuelan President "Hurricane Hugo" Chavez came to the UN and put down President Bush—that our "Commander in Chief" didn't respond with humor.

YIKES! He let a perfect opportunity go by and should've retorted on the news that night by saying...

"As you know President Chavez was here recently and made some disparaging comments about my character. I will take the high road and wish him only the best as he visits our free and open society.… Oh, and as he dines out tonight might I recommend he have the Spinach salad!"

To effectively use current events you are in essence capturing "lightning in a bottle." Humor when applied correctly can hit a target like no other weapon—especially when it's in the audience's collective memory. Read the papers daily and see what two current events you can bring together for optimal results.

Once you train yourself to do this... it will almost become second nature to you. I guarantee it!

Keep laughing!

Peter "The Humorator" Fogel

www.fortune500comedy.com

P.S. Please pass this e-zine on to anyone who can benefit from it. I will thank you … and so will they.

I am headlining "Catch a Rising Star" at Resorts International in Atlantic City, Oct 7th through the 14th. If you're in the area please stop by, see the show—and say "hi"!

Peter "The Humorator" Fogel's Guide to Effective Public Speaking
www.fortune500comedy.com/PublicSpeakingEBook/index.html

"If Not Now … Then When? Stories

And Strategies of People Over 40 Who
Successfully Reinvented Themselves
by Peter Fogel

www.buybooksontheweb.com/description.asp?ISBN=0-7414-2401-0
Comedy CD
Almost Live From NYC It's The Comedy of Peter "The Humor" Fogel
www.fortune500comedy.com/products.html#Want

(I pay shipping and handling on comedy CD)
Fortune 500 Comedy Communications
8350 Sunrise Lakes Blvd.
Sunrise, Florida 33322
USA

If you no longer wish to receive communication from us:
http://autocontactor.com/app/r.asp?ID=87231344&ARID=0

To update your contact information:
http://autocontactor.com/app/r.asp?c=1&ID=87231344

Sample E-zine #2
Pam Lontos's "PR/PR PULSE"

From: newsletter@prpr.net
To: Roscoe Barnes
Date: Mon, 18 Sep 2006
PR/PR PULSE

Welcome to "PR/PR Pulse," a free e-zine provided by PR/PR. Your complimentary issue will give you tips to get the print, radio, TV, and Internet publicity that you and your business deserve!

If you wish to opt-out of this service, please send an email to newsletter@prpr.net with "Unsubscribe" in the subject line.

PR/PR Pulse
Publisher: Pam Lontos
www.prpr.net
Phone: 407-299-6128
Fax: 407-299-2166
Email: newsletter@prpr.net

Tips and Tools for Better Publicity for Your Book, Business, Speaking and Self! Please forward this e-zine to anyone you know who needs insider tips on how to generate free publicity. If you'd like to send a comment, suggestion or ask a question to be answered in the newsletter, please email: newsletter@prpr.net.

This Month's Issue

1. Maximize Your Exposure by Building Relationships with Media
2. This Month's Publicity Events/Opportunities
3. This Month's Inspiring Quote
4. Have a Need for Publicity?

1. Maximize Your Exposure by Building Relationships with the Media

You already know that the media is the best avenue for promoting your business because it adds credibility to your message, positions you as the expert, and best of all…it's free. So you've done a few interviews and gotten quoted in a few articles, but those just left you hungry for more.

Now, how do you expand on the contacts you've already made? The key to getting more exposure is to build relationships with the media professionals.

Use these tips on giving excellent interviews to start building your relationships with the media:

Most of your interviews will take place over the phone, but that doesn't mean you don't have to give a good first impression. Yes, you can wear jeans and a sweatshirt but you can't sound incompetent. When the reporter can't see you, they will draw all their conclusions about you from your tone of voice and your word choices.

Here are more tips on building relationships with the media:

- ▶ Before the interview, prepare for the call. Take time and write down the main points to cover. Use this as an opportunity to relax, collect your thoughts, and make a few notes. Avoid reading scripted responses from a pre-printed sheet. You want to sound natural and honest. Also, seek a quiet spot for the interview. If your office is noisy and busy, close yourself off in a room without distractions. With a few notes ready and all your distractions put away, you won't struggle through the interview; you'll sound relaxed and confident.

- ▶ When the phone rings and the interview starts, stand up and smile while you talk. Standing, like you're giving a live presentation, raises your energy level and you'll be more alert than if you were sitting. Additionally, a genuine smile radiates through the phone line, and the reporter on the other end will feel the joy in your voice.

- ▶ Be respectful and show the reporter that you care. Ask them if you're talking too quickly, because reporters always take notes by hand. Also, ask nicely if they will mention your business information. Don't be pushy; remember, the reporter decides how much room you get in their story. And never request a copy of the story for your approval. The reporter doesn't answer to you. But don't be afraid to show interest by asking for a copy of the magazine or a tape of the show after publication or broadcast.

- ▶ As the interview starts to wrap up, inquire about other stories the reporter is currently covering. Explain how you may be able to add to them and offer a unique angle that may interest their audience. Let the reporter know that they can call you back if they have any questions, or provide them with other sources. And show them that you're eager to be an accessible source of information in the future.

For more publicity tips, visit our web site: *www.prpr.net*

"I attribute the effective use of well-placed PR to much of my success. I have never endorsed or recommended a firm with this level of excitement, but Pam Lontos, the owner of PR/PR, is a keeper."

—Sy Sperling, Founder of Hair Club for Men

2. Publicity Events for the Month of October

If your expertise fits any of these topics, take advantage by sending out a press release to newspaper, television and radio stations, or call up the media directly!

For example, because October is Diversity Month, those who have expertise in dealing with diversity issues in the workplace should send out a press release or media alert to newspapers a week or two prior to October. In it, you should provide them with reasons on how your expertise can benefit their readers. You may want to include topics that you can discuss such as how to manage a diverse workplace or hire a diverse group of employees.

- ▶ October is Diversity Awareness Month—A month to celebrate, promote and appreciate the diversity of our society. This month also includes furthering the understanding of the values of all races, genders, nationalities, age groups, religions, physical disabilities, and sexual orientation.
- ▶ October is Self-Promotion Month—Designated as such to push individuals to learn how to promote themselves and/or their businesses to another level of success.
- ▶ October is Women's Small Business Month—Celebrating the success, determination, and independence of these women and their businesses.
- ▶ The first week in October is National Work from Home Week—A week to celebrate the trends, technology, and tactics that allow millions of Americans to work from home.
- ▶ The second week in October is National Networking Week—Promoting the importance of networking to grow your business through meeting new people, exchanging business cards, and sharing your goals and desires with other people.
- ▶ The third week in October is Achieving Financial Independence Week—A week dedicated to making people, at any life stage, aware of ways to achieve financial independence.
- ▶ October 9th is Columbus Day
- ▶ October 16th is National Boss Day
- ▶ October 31st is Halloween

3. This Month's "Inspirational" Quote

"Cherish your visions and your dreams, as they are the children of your soul, the blueprints of your ultimate achievements."

—Napoleon Hill

This Month Our Clients Have Been Interviewed by or Featured in:

- ▶ *Time:* Dr. Andrew Edelman on Quirky Niche Consultants
- ▶ *USA Today:* Dr. Ron Knaus on Feeling Sleepy at Work
- ▶ *New York Times:* Phil Wilkins on Declining a Promotion
- ▶ *Human Resource Executive:* Don Schmincke on CEOs and Talent Management
- ▶ *First for Women:* Paul Kowal on Getting What You Want in Customer Service
- ▶ *Christian Science Monitor:* Francie Dalton on Have You Ever Been Fired?

- *Entrepreneur:* Laura Leist on the Top 10 Entrepreneurs' New Year's Resolutions
- *New York Times*: Laura Rikleen on Declining a Promotion
- *Star Magazine:* The Passing Zone on Celebrity Mistakes
- *Bottom Line/Personal:* Peter D'Arruda on Investment Experts
- *Selling Power:* Marc Freeman on Re-negotiation
- *Woman's Day:* Dr. Ron Knaus on Exercises for Older Women
- *Lavalife.com:* Dr. Molly Barrow on How to Avoid Dating a Jerk
- Tribune Media Services: Dr. Maurice Ramirez on Adjusting to a New Schedule
- *First for Women:* Dr. Christopher Knippers on How to Talk to Anyone

4. Have a Need for Publicity?

PR/PR can help you with all of your publicity needs, from print to television, radio and online media. If you want to sell more books, get more speaking engagements and be hired for more consulting jobs, you need publicity.
To receive a free consultation, please contact Pam Lontos, President of PR/PR: 407-299-6128 or via email at: pam@prpr.net.

Unleash Your Inner Author ...

RESOURCE FOR BOOK WRITING, PUBLISHING, AND PROMOTING.
Dan Poynter's F-R-E-E e-zine:
http://parapublishing.com/sites/para/resources/newsletter.cfm

Need Help Marketing Your Book?

Get free book-marketing tips every other week in Brian Jud's book Marketing Matters e-newsletter. Go to: www.bookmarketing.com to sign up!
Permission to reprint: You may reprint any items from "PR/PR Pulse" in your own print or electronic newsletter, but please include the following:

"Reprinted from "PR/PR Pulse," a free e-zine featuring tips and techniques for gaining publicity. To receive this e-zine, please send an email to newsletter@prpr.net with "Add Me" in the subject line.

If you like any of the advice from this e-zine, please pass this on to your friends, clients and colleagues.

We would love to hear from you! Please email your suggestions and/or questions about publicity to: newsletter@prpr.net.

PR/PR
President: Pam Lontos
775 S. Kirkman Road, Suite 104
Orlando, FL 32811
www.prpr.net
Phone: 407-299-6128
Fax: 407-299-2166

Pam Lontos is the president of PR/PR, a public relations firm that specializes in professional speakers, authors and experts. An author, speaker, and former VP of Disney's Shamrock Broadcasting, Pam knows the ropes of getting good you publicity and how to use it to boost your bookings or book sales. Call for a free consultation at (407) 299-6128 or visit: www.prpr.net.

If you no longer wish to receive this e-zine, please email: newsletter@prpr.net and include "Unsubscribe" in the subject line.

Sample Ezine #3

Beth Ann Erickson's "Writing Etc."

Writing Etc.—October 1, 2006

ISSN: 1545-5580

Tips, Techniques, and Resources to Transform You from an Average Freelancer to a Highly Paid Professional

To subscribe to Writing Etc. and receive the free e-book, "Power Queries," surf here: http://filbertpublishing.com

Hey, did you know you can get your hands on 150+ webpages of free writing info? Just head to http://FilbertPublishing.com and dig around. You can also visit our High Profit Writing Vault by clicking the link below. Enjoy!

Forward Writing Etc. to all your writing friends! They'll be glad you did.

For easier reading and red hot links, surf to
ttp://filbertpublishing.com/current.html
Your Key to the High Profit Writing vault is here: http://filbertpublishing.com/Top_Secret_Vault.html

Notes from Minnesota: Please allow me to introduce little Jake the Agony and the Ecstasy by Beth Ann Erickson

- ▶ Paying Markets
- ▶ Cool Announcement
- ▶ Highly Recommended
- ▶ Four years in the making. Information like none other.
- ▶ Over 101 battle-tested techniques to utterly turbo-charge your freelance income.
- ▶ Now available as an extremely affordable, instantly downloadable e-book.

Get all the juicy details here: http://filbertpublishing.com/101.html

Greetings from Minnesota!

July 5, 2006. I'm still reeling over the death of my "Lucy the Rat Terrier Wonder Dog" when the phone rings.

"Are you done crying about Lu yet?"

"Nope," I reply.

"Well get over it," the voice on the other side of the line says.

"You've gotta get in here. Now."

Read the rest here: http://filbertpublishing.com/current.html

Feature Article
The Agony and the Ecstasy
By Beth Ann Erickson

I entered the freelance world with visions of lazy afternoons, muse-filled evenings, and productive mornings.

Reality?

A little different. Actually quite different.

Running a successful writing business can take more time than you expect, chew through your muse faster than you can say "novel" and take you places you never expected.

Let me explain.

In case you don't know, I write advertising copy to finance my "novel writing habit." It's a fair trade off with fiction writing satisfying my creative outlet and copywriting providing the income I need to (more than) pay the bills, finance my many travels, and keep Cutie Rudie and Jake the Min Pin in trendy puppy sweaters.

Everything rolls along smooth … usually.

What do you have to do with all this? Check it out here:

http://filbertpublishing.com/current.html

Paying Markets—http://filbertpublishing.com/current.html

Quick Announcements and a Rumor!

Want to earn a 50 percent commission on every book you sell? http://filbertpublishing.com/current.html

Feel free to forward Writing Etc. to all your writing friends. Just be sure to include the entire issue. Thanks!

We strive to make Writing Etc. an invaluable resource to writers. If you have any comments or suggestions please send them to: filbertpublishing@filbertpublishing.com

For Easier Reading and Red Hot URLs, read this issue online at: http://filbertpublishing.com/current.html

The Fine Print

You are receiving this e-mag because you (or someone who has access to your computer/e-mail account) entered your e-mail address into our subscription form at http://filbertpublishing.com AND confirmed your desire to receive this fre* subscription via e-mail.

If you feel you are receiving this publication in error, we want to know about it. E-mail us at filbertpublishing(a)filbertpublishing.com so we can investigate how your e-mail address arrived into our double-opt-in system. Also, you can easily remove your e-mail addy from this list at any time by clicking your personalized link at the end of this e-mail.

To receive Writing, Etc. surf to http://filbertpublishing.com and insert your e-mail address into the form.

Please recommend this newsletter to anyone you know who'd like to learn how to make their writing sparkle.

PRIVACY STATEMENT: We will not distribute your e-mail address to anyone. Ever. Period.

Writing Etc.
Box 326
Kandiyohi, MN 56251
Maurice and Beth Erickson, Publishers
filbertpublishing(a)filbertpublishing.com
http://filbertpublishing.com/
© 2006 Filbert Publishing

Flbert Publishing, 140 3rd S , Kandiyohi, MN 56251, USA
To unsubscribe or change subscriber options visit:
http://www.aweber.com/z/r/?TOxMjCwctCwMzBwsTMys

Sample Ezine #4

Robert W. Bly's "Direct Response Letter"

To: mailings@bly.com

Subject: Does print advertising still work?

Date: Tue, 31 Oct 2006 10:08:36 -0500

From: Bob Bly mailings@bly.com

Bob Bly's Direct Response Letter: Resources, ideas, and tips for improving response to business-to-business, high-tech, and direct marketing.

November 2006

You are getting this e-mail because you subscribed to it on www.bly.com or because you are one of Bob's clients, prospects, seminar attendees, or book buyers. If you would prefer not to receive further e-mails of this type, go to www.bly.com, enter your e-mail address, and hit Unsubscribe.

Your subscription brings you one regular monthly issue, usually at the beginning of the month, plus one or two supplementary messages each week, usually recommendations for information on products on marketing and related topics. I review each product personally before endorsing them and in many cases know the authors.

We do not rent or share your name with anybody. Feel free to forward this issue to any peers, friends and associates you think would benefit from its contents. They will thank you. So will I.

Success Without Stress

What follows is not directly related to marketing, writing, and the other topics I typically cover in this newsletter—and it is easy to dismiss advice like this as simplistic or trivial. But when copywriter Kim Stacey e-mailed this list to me, I read it carefully—and found it to be deceptively profound and effective.

Here are 10 tips for living less stressfully, from "Loving and Leaving the Good Life" by Helen Nearing:

1. Do the best you can, whatever arises.
2. Be at peace with yourself.
3. Find a job you enjoy.
4. Live in simple conditions; get rid of clutter.
5. Contact nature every day; find the earth under your feet.
6. Take physical exercise.
7. Don't worry; live one day at a time.
8. Share something every day with someone else; help someone else somehow.

9. Take time to wonder at the world and at life; see some humor in life where you can.

10. Be kind.

Do Print Ads Work for Lead Generation?

Yes, according to research from the Advertising Research Foundation (ARF).

According to ARF, two out of every three people responding to ads have real needs.

The rest—commonly called "brochure collectors"—presumably just like sending for sales literature and collecting free information.

But are ad leads valuable?

Yes. ARF says that one out of every five leads generated by advertising converts into a sale for the product.

Source: *Metalworking Marketer*, 10/06, p. 3.

Why There Are No Rules in DM

Conventional wisdom says, "Showing a picture of your premium will lift response."

But the other day, I spoke with a marketing director who says he tested this—and found that showing a picture of their premium (a free booklet) actually depressed response.

And many years ago, I met a directory publisher who swore that when he tested removing the 30-day money-back guarantee from his mailing, it did not depress response one bit.

More proof that no rules are inviolate and the only way to know what will work for you is to test.

10 Easy Steps to Landing Lucrative Corporate Clients

My friend and colleague Chris Marlow, whom some of you may know as a marketing coach for freelancers, has just put elements of her successful self-marketing system into a Special Report you can get for free. Until now, the only view into her self-marketing system was held by those who committed to her coaching program.

Chris's new report, "10 Steps to Landing the High-Quality, High-Paying Corporate Clients," can be instantly downloaded when you sign up for the *Freelancer's Business Bulletin*, an excellent monthly newsletter on landing high-profile clients.

To sign up for the *Freelancer's Business Bulletin* and get your FREE instant download of "10 Steps to Landing the High-Quality, High-Paying Corporate Clients," visit www.freelancersbusinessbulletin.com.

Bob Bly on Copywriting"—Tours Free!

Michael Senoff recently interviewed me for a 2-hour, wide-ranging discussion on copywriting, marketing, freelancing, the writing life, and related topics. If you read and enjoy this e-newsletter, I'm pretty sure you'll find this conversation fascinating—even useful. To hear it or download a PDF transcript, just click below now: www.hardtofindseminars.com/Copywriting.html#Bob%20Bly

3 Ways to Sell More Subscriptions

1. Use department store pricing—$9.97 instead of $10.
2. Include a "no" option—yes/no options help to eliminate inertia and add credibility to time-limited offers.
3. Test sweepstakes, stickers, tokens, scratch-offs, and other such devices—they may transform a modest-selling promo into a winning control.

Source: "More Dos and Don'ts to Help Maximize Subscriptions," Subscription Marketing, Vol. 13, No. 4, p.14.

Joke of the Month

A traveling salesman was driving uphill through a rural area when he spotted something he'd never been before—a three-legged chicken—running at blazing speed on the side of the road. He tried to pull his car closer to get a better view, but when he did, to his surprise, the chicken put on a burst of speed—outpacing the car and disappearing over the top of the hill. When the salesman crested the hill, he saw a farmer standing there with a pitchfork, a barn, and a farmhouse behind him. He asked the farmer whether he'd seen the amazing three-legged chicken.

"'Course I have," said the farmer. "I breed them!"

When the salesman asked why, the farmer replied: "Simple. I like a drumstick … wife likes a drumstick … and my boy likes a drumstick."

"How do the three-legged chickens taste?" the salesman asked.

"Dunno," replied the farmer. "Never caught one."

Speak, Sell, and Grow Rich

If you're a consultant, small business owner, coach, author, salesperson or marketer, one of the quickest and most efficient ways for you to get a targeted audience clamoring for your products or services—not to mention making you an expert in their eyes—is through effective public speaking.

Now, my good friend Peter "The Humorator" Fogel—a successful speaker and stand-up comic—invites you to take the first step toward public speaking prowess and sign up for his FREE e-course, "7 Days to Effective Public Speaking."
For more information, click below now:
www.fortune500comedy.com/PublicSpeakingEBook/bly.html

Quotation of the Month

"… it had been a winter of deadening seriousness, when all the illusions and bright dreams of my early twenties had withered and died. I did not yet have the interior resources to dream new dreams; I was far too busy mourning the death of the old ones and wondering how I was going to survive without them. I was sure I could replace them somehow, but was not sure I could restore their brassy luster or dazzling impress."

—Pat Conroy, *The Prince of Tides* (Houghton Mifflin, 1986)

60-Second Commercial from Fern Dickey, Project Manager

Bob is available on a limited basis for copywriting of direct mail packages, sales letters, brochures, white papers, ads, e-mail marketing campaigns, PR materials, and Web pages. We recommend you call for a FREE copy of our updated Copywriting Information Kit. Just let us know your industry and the type of copy you're interested in seeing (ads, mailings, etc.), and if Bob is available to take your assignment, we'll tailor a package of recent samples to fit your requirements. Call Fern Dickey at 201-797-8105 or e-mail fern1128@optonline.net.

Bob Bly
Copywriter/consultant
22 E. Quackenbush Ave.
Dumont, NJ 07628
phone 201-385-1220
fax 201-385-1138
rwbly@bly.com
www.bly.com

Mailings mailing list
Mailings@bly.com

If you would like to unsubscribe from this mailing list, follow the instructions under "Unsubscribing from Mailings" at the following link: www.bly.com/mailman/options/mailings/roscoebarnes3%40yahoo.com.

Index

About the Author

Roscoe Barnes III is an award-winning journalist, ghostwriter and a nationally known copywriter who specializes in direct response marketing for non-profit organizations. When he's not busy writing copy for contributions, he writes direct mail packages and publicity copy for consumer and business-to-business markets. He also works as a publicity consultant.

Barnes has written copy for such national non-profit clients as the World Bible Translation Center, Lautman & Co., and Good News Jail & Prison Ministry, among others. His commercial clients have consisted of scores of small businesses, including LA Weight-Loss Center.

Prolific and Versatile

Barnes has been dubbed a "Renaissance Writer" because of the different types of writing that he does. Since he began writing in 1982, he has established himself as an award-winning journalist, a columnist, a religious writer, a pastor and prison chaplain, an Army veteran, seminar leader, artist, book publisher and a marketing consultant for small businesses. He is a correspondent for Publishers' Auxiliary, the official publication of the National Newspaper Association.

Nationally known Columnist

Barnes is a former columnist for two national publications: Fund Raising Management magazine (Hoke Communications Inc.), where he wrote "Copy Thoughts"; and Publishers Auxiliary (National Newspaper Association), where he wrote "Streetwise Reporting." He currently writes a monthly column for *Tidal Wave Business News Magazine*.

His work has been featured in a number of popular business books, including *Secrets of a Freelance Writer* and *The Complete Idiot's Guide to Direct Marketing*, *Secrets of Successful Telephone Selling*, all by Robert W. Bly; and *The AMA's* (American Marketing Association) *Complete Guide to Small Business Advertising* by Joe Vitale.

Author of Numerous Books and Gospel Tracts

Barnes is the author of numerous books and training guides, the subjects of which span everything from World War II history and journalism to self-help and art. The titles include: *Direct Response Advertising Made Easy* (Entrepreneur Press, 2007) *The Better Letter: Essential Tips for Effective Fundraising Copy* (Target Marketing Group/NAPCO, 2006), *Mighty Through God: Biography of Dr. G.D. Voorhis* (editor,

Dr. G.D. Voorhis Educational Program Inc., 2006), *The Guide to Effective Gospel Tract Ministry* (Church Growth Institute, 2004), *Secrets of a Writing Hustler: How to Beat the Odds—Overcome Rejection—and Succeed as a Writer* (Filbert Publishing, 2005), *Off to War: Franklin Countians in World War II* (White Mane Publishing, 1996), *Bicentennial: Our People, Our Heritage* (contributor, The Record Herald, 1997), *Discover Your Talent and Find Fulfillment* (McKinley & Henson, 1992), *Big Bucks from Little Sketches* (McKinley & Henson, 1993), *Scooping the Competition: How to Be FIRST in Reporting HOT Stories* (Roscoe Barnes/National Newspaper Association, 1998).

Barnes is also the author of many gospel tracts (religious pamphlets) which are published by some of the leading Christian publishing houses: The Tract League, Christian Light Publications, Herald Press, Pilgrim Tract Society, and Grace & Truth. Winner of Journalism Awards

As a journalist, Barnes has worked for both military and civilian newspapers. In 1985, after working for *The Enterprise-Tocsin* (Indianola, Miss.), the Mississippi Press Association awarded him First Place honors for Best Investigative Reporting. In 1996, while writing for The Record Herald (Waynesboro, Pa.), the Pennsylvania Newspaper Publishers' Association awarded him Second Place honors for Best News Beat Reporting. That same year, he took honorable mentions for Best Spot News Story and his newsroom was named Newsroom of the Year in a national contest sponsored by American Publishing Company.

Barnes has published articles, book reviews, news stories and features in trade, military and inspirational magazines. He has published fiction in literary magazines in the United States and Germany. He last worked as a full-time journalist for *Public Opinion*, a Gannett-owned daily newspaper in Chambersburg, PA.

Widely Published in Magazines and Newspapers.

In addition to The Associated Press and many state press associations, Barnes has written for: *Editor & Publisher, EurArmy, Grace in Focus, Church of God Evangel, Pentecostal Evangel, Lighted Pathway, Refleks Journal, Grit, Writers' Forum,* Authorship, Writers Journal, HomeBusiness Magazine, Grace & Truth Magazine, *Enrichment Journal, Pulpit Helps, Soldier, Command, BodyTalk, The Cracker Barrel Magazine, Elizabethtown Magazine,* and *At Ease.* His work has also appeared on the pages of *The Washington Post, Current Thoughts & Trends, The Patriot News* (Harrisburg, PA), and a number of other newspapers and magazines.

Ph.D. Student/Seminary Graduate

In terms of his educational background, Barnes is currently pursuing a Ph.D. in church history through the University of Pretoria, South Africa. He has completed graduate work with Boston University and holds a Master of Arts degree from Lutheran Theological Seminary (Gettysburg, Pa.). He earned his Bachelor of Science and Associate of Science degrees (Cum Laude) from East Coast Bible College/Lee University-Charlotte Center (Charlotte, N.C.) He is a graduate of the Christian Writers Guild.

Seminar Leader and College Lecturer

A native of Indianola, MS, Barnes has taught writing and communication courses for the University of Maryland (Germany) and Harrisburg (PA) Area Community College. He has led workshops and seminars for the Mississippi Press Association, the Pennsylvania Women's Press Association and the New York Press Association, among other groups.